Paul and the Historical Jesus

David Wenham

Lecturer in New Testament, Wycliffe Hall, Oxford

GROVE BOOKS LIMITED
RIDLEY HALL RD CAMBRIDGE CB3 9HU

Contents

The Cover Illustration is by Peter Ashton

First Impression March 1998
ISSN 1365-490X
ISBN 1 85174 369 3

1
Introduction

St Paul was perhaps the most effective Christian evangelist the world has ever seen, and his letters, which we find in the New Testament, are usually regarded as the earliest Christian writings that we have (1 Thessalonians, for example, was written less than twenty years after Jesus' death, in about AD 49, and Galatians perhaps even earlier. The gospels were probably written a good few years later). You might expect, therefore, that Paul would be one of the most valuable and important witnesses that we have to the historical Jesus.[1] In fact, however, Paul is often seen as a hindrance rather than a help by modern Christians trying to explain the Christian faith.

Three things are often said about Paul and the gospel traditions, which Christians have found problematic.

1 'Paul preached a different gospel from Jesus'

Many hold that Paul's own religious faith and ideas were significantly different from those of Jesus. Jesus, so it is said, was simply a Galilean prophet or wise man, who called people to repentance and faith in God. But Paul introduced all sorts of dogma into the simple religion of Jesus, making Jesus out to be a divine figure and Son of God and replacing Jesus' emphasis on the kingdom or rule of God with much more abstruse ideas about being justified through Jesus' sacrificial death. It is also held that Paul exchanged Jesus' advanced social ideas (for example his positive world-affirming outlook, and his views on the equality of women and men) with much more conventional and negative views of the body, of sex, of women and of social justice. Paul may describe himself as a 'slave of Jesus Christ,' but he was actually influenced by all sorts of things other than Jesus, including religious ideas from the Greek culture of his time and his own mystical experiences. The result is a significantly different religion from that of Jesus, and, as A N Wilson[2] and many others before him have argued, Paul rather than Jesus is the founder of Christianity as we know it.

2 'Some of the Gospel stories about Jesus were invented later by the church'

It is often argued that Paul puts a big historical question mark against important gospel accounts of Jesus' life and in particular his birth and

---

1   Even if Paul did not meet Jesus himself, he was around Jerusalem very soon after the time of Jesus.
2   *Paul: The Mind of the Apostle* (London: Sinclair-Stevenson, 1997) p 258.

resurrection. Paul's failure even to mention the Christmas stories about Mary, Joseph and the baby Jesus is thought to confirm that those stories reflect a late development in Christian thinking about Jesus, rather than very early tradition. It is true that Paul confidently affirms the reality of Jesus' resurrection. But (a) he appears to be completely ignorant of the stories about the women finding the empty tomb, which are primary in all the gospels, and (b) he lists himself with the witnesses of the risen Jesus, thus making it clear in some people's view that he sees the resurrection appearances as visionary, like his own vision of the risen Christ on the Damascus Road. The conclusion reached from this evidence, for example recently by the German scholar Gerd Lüdemann, is that the idea of Jesus' resurrection arose first out of a visionary experience of one or more of the disciples and that the notion of an empty tomb came in later, when the Christians wished to defend themselves against the charge that the resurrection was a figment of their imagination (or hallucinations).[3]

3 'The early Christians were not interested in the history of Jesus'

More generally Paul's striking failure to refer much to the life of Jesus in his letters is thought to demonstrate that the earliest Christians were not very interested in the history of Jesus. They were interested in the presence of the risen Christ in their Christian communities and in the prospect of his return from heaven, but not much in his past (except for his symbolically significant death and resurrection). Thus Paul, who can refer so often to the Old Testament, has just a tiny handful of proven references to Jesus' life and teaching;[4] he has no unambiguous references to Jesus' miracles, his exorcisms, his parables, or to almost anything else. If this lack of interest is typical of the early Christians, then it has serious implications for anyone concerned about what actually happened in Jesus' life and ministry. It confirms the views of those critics who argue that there was no sustained attempt in the earliest days of the church to preserve the stories of Jesus—the gospels are more the testimony of faith than accounts of what happened. Paul's evidence thus puts in question not only important gospel traditions (such as Jesus' infancy and resurrection) but the *whole* of the tradition. The conclusion of this view is that the historian must treat the gospels with caution, if not scepticism.

To what extent are these three arguments about Paul and the historical Jesus true and persuasive?[5] To what extent are they a reflection of a 20th century

---

3 *The Resurrection of Jesus* (London: SCM, 1994).
4 Notably 1 Cor 7.10 on divorce, and 1 Cor 9.14 on the evangelist deserving payment.
5 If the third argument about Paul's lack of interest in the traditions of Jesus' ministry is true, then the force of the second argument about his failure to mention the infancy narratives is arguably diminished.

liberalism, which finds a dogma-free Jesus who challenged the *status quo* more appealing than a divine Jesus who was born of a virgin and who rose physically out of a tomb?[6] We will comment on each in turn.

2

Is Paul's Theology Different from that of Jesus?

Paul's Understanding of Jesus as Son of God

There is no question that Paul had a very high view of Jesus as Son of God, and it is likely that a major contributory factor in his understanding was his Damascus Road experience of the risen Lord. But this experience, though decisive in the development of his own thinking, was not the origin of the idea of Jesus as Son of God. Indeed the idea goes back to Jesus himself. The decisive evidence in favour of this is the use of the Aramaic word 'Abba' in Mark's gospel and in Paul's letters to the Galatians and the Romans. Mark describes Jesus in Gethsemane crying in prayer 'Abba, Father, let this cup pass from me,' and Paul in Galatians 4.6, and Romans 8.15, describes Christians also as crying 'Abba.' It is easy for us to miss the oddness of Paul writing in Greek to Greek-speaking readers and describing the Christian cry as 'Abba' (in Aramaic). But the obvious explanation is that the cry goes back to Jesus, for whom Aramaic was almost certainly his first language, and that it became a specially treasured part of the Christian tradition.[7] Experts in first-century Judaism have noted how 'Abba' was the normal way for members of families to address their father, but not a normal way for Jews to address God. It seems that the usage was something distinctive of Jesus, and so it imprinted itself even in the traditions of the Greek-speaking church.[8]

As well as the 'Abba' cry of Jesus, Paul probably knew other sayings of

---

6 It is a commonplace that in the 'quest for the historical Jesus' scholars have come up with pictures of Jesus that look like mirror images of their own preferences! This should not cause us to despair of historical research, but should remind us that arguments may gain currency because of their subjective appeal rather than because of their objective cogency, as well as alert us to our own prejudices!

7 This explanation is suggested both by Mark's description of Jesus in Gethsemane, and also by Paul who sees the Christian cry as the work of the Spirit of Jesus in the believer: see Gal 4.6 on 'the Spirit of his Son...crying "Abba! Father!"'

8 To say that the idea of Jesus as Son of God goes back to Jesus' own self-understanding is not to say that Paul's understanding and Jesus' understanding were identical. Paul's understanding was surely coloured by his own experience on the Damascus Road, as well as by his convictions concerning the death and resurrection of Jesus. Nevertheless, Paul was clearly not the originator of this important idea.

Jesus where he speaks of himself as Son of God, as in Matthew 11.25–27/ Luke 10.21–22: 'I thank you, Father, Lord of heaven and earth, that you have hidden these things from the wise and understanding and revealed them to babes; yes, Father, for such was your gracious will. All things have been delivered to me by my Father; and no one knows the Son except the Father, and no one knows the Father except the Son and anyone to whom the Son chooses to reveal him.'[9] Paul uses various of the same ideas and phrases in 1 Corinthians 1 and 2 when responding to Christians in Corinth who were boasting of their spiritual wisdom ('hidden,' 'wisdom of the wise,' 'the understanding,' 'revealed,' 'babes,' 'God was pleased').[10] The similarity of the ideas is unlikely to be coincidental.

Paul may well have known Jesus' parable of the vineyard tenants (Matt 21.33–34 and parallels), in which Jesus describes the master sending his son to get the fruits of the vineyard, only to be killed by the tenants. Thus Paul can refer to God 'sending his Son' in the fullness of time, in order to die.[11] Paul may also have known the tradition of Jesus' baptism. Certainly the way that he describes Christian baptism—as a watery ritual, which brings the believer into sonship and into an experience of the Holy Spirit—is strikingly reminiscent of the gospel accounts of Jesus' baptism.

Some of these parallels prove rather little by themselves, and we must be careful of what someone has called 'parallelomania,' making a great deal out of parallels that may not actually be very significant.[12] But, even if some of the evidence is only in the category of what is 'possible,' we have in the use of 'Abba' one very strong piece of evidence that Paul got his understanding of Jesus as Son of God from the stories and sayings of Jesus.

Jesus as Lord

Much more important for Paul than the idea of Jesus as Son of God was the idea of Jesus as 'Lord.' Once again the evidence shows that this was not an idea original to Paul. It is another Aramaic word that shows this, since at the end of 1 Corinthians Paul again drops into Aramaic without warning, when he writes 'Maranatha' (16.22). This is probably a prayer meaning 'Our Lord, come,' and the use of the Aramaic word suggests that we have a prayer that was important in the earliest Aramaic liturgical traditions of the church, as they eagerly awaited the Lord's return. So again we have a significant

---

9 Many scholars would trace these sayings back to the hypothetical 'Q' source supposedly used by Matthew and Luke. For bibliographical details on this and other points, see my full-length treatment of the Jesus-Paul question, *Paul: Follower of Jesus or Founder or Christianity?* (Grand Rapids: Eerdmans, 1995).

10 1 Cor 2.7, 1.19, 2.10, 3.1, 1.21.

11 Gal 4.4, Rom 8.3.

12 For the term 'parallelomania' see S Sandmel in *Journal of Biblical Literature* 81 (1962) 1–13. On the question of method see further below.

way of referring to Jesus that antedates Paul. 'Jesus is Lord' may well have been the earliest Christian confession, used in baptismal contexts[13] and used also in the Aramaic church before Paul's time.

Where did the church get this idea from? No doubt the resurrection persuaded them once and for all that Jesus was Lord (Acts 2.36), but the gospels point to the church getting the idea originally from Jesus himself. According to Matthew 22.41–45 Jesus asked his opponents one of his typically enigmatic and challenging questions, about Psalm 110.1, 'The Lord said to my Lord…' The subtle thrust of Jesus' question is a claim on Jesus' part to be not only Son of David but also David's Lord.

The Death of the Lord

The idea of Jesus' death as a saving sacrifice is, of course, of the greatest importance to Paul, and he might conceivably have developed the idea himself after his conversion experience. After all, how would you make sense of the death of God's Messiah, if you were a well-trained Jew like Paul and if you had had a Damascus Road experience? The death could hardly have been accident; it must have been in the purposes of God, and the logical explanation would surely be in terms of Old Testament sacrifice and Jewish martyr theology. Paul could have developed his theology of Jesus' atonement in that way, perhaps helped by the Greek mystery religions, with their dying and rising deities. But the evidence is that, once again, the root of Paul's understanding of the death of the Lord lies with Jesus himself.

The evidence in question is in 1 Corinthians 11.23–26, where Paul describes the Lord's supper, introducing it as follows: 'for I received from the Lord what I also delivered to you, that the Lord Jesus on the night when he was betrayed took bread…' Three things at least are notable about this: (1) that Paul uses a form of words that was conventionally used for the transmission of tradition ('received…delivered'); (2) that Paul speaks of himself having received traditions and then passing them on to the Corinthians, and (3) that the traditions in question in this passage are familiar to us from the gospels. This evidence is significant in many ways, not least because it shows that Paul was familiar with what we know as the gospel stories of Jesus (or some of them) and that he taught them in the churches that he founded. But for our present purposes all we are particularly concerned to observe is that Paul received a tradition of the Lord's supper, which expressed a highly significant theology of the death of the Lord: the tradition spoke of Jesus' death being 'for you' ('my body for you…') and it included sacrificial ideas of 'new covenant' and 'blood' ('this cup is the new covenant in my blood'). Later in 1 Corinthians 15, where Paul again speaks of tradition being received and

---

13 See 1 Cor 12.3, Rom 10.9.

passed on, he also speaks of Christ 'dying for our sins, according to the Scriptures' (15.3). He does not specify the Scriptures concerned, but we may be sure that they included the Old Testament Scriptures about sacrifice and covenant (for example Exodus 24), and we may surmise with considerable confidence that they included also the Passover texts. Paul does not describe the Lord's supper as a Passover meal, as do the synoptics, but the way that he says in 1 Corinthians 5.7, 'Christ our Passover lamb has been sacrificed for us' shows that he takes for granted this understanding of Jesus' death.[14]

Paul, therefore, did not create the idea of Jesus' atoning death, with or without the help of the mystery religions. He may have developed it in various ways, but it was a given for him—a given firmly rooted in the ministry of Jesus, in his final meal with his disciples in Jerusalem at Passover time just before his death.

Within the synoptic gospels the two most significant sayings of Jesus relating to his death are the last supper tradition that we have discussed, and the teaching of Jesus about servanthood, which climaxes in the saying of Jesus, 'For the Son of man came not to be served, but to serve and to give his life as a ransom for many' (Mark 10.45). It is not possible to prove that Paul was familiar with this tradition of Jesus, but he does refer very powerfully to Jesus as the humble servant (for example in Philippians 2), and he also refers to his own imitation of Jesus in making himself the servant of all (1 Cor 9.19–23, 10.33–11.1). It is a reasonable guess that Paul has been influenced by the sayings of Jesus in question; in the case of the last supper traditions it is much more than a guess.[15]

The Ethics of Jesus and Paul

If Paul is less creative in his views on the meaning of Jesus Christ's life and death than has often been supposed, what about his ethics? Has he abandoned Jesus' socially radical ideas for something less?

---

14 Compare also 1 Cor 10 for Exodus motifs in 1 Corinthians.

15 Despite this evidence, it might still be argued that Paul's emphasis on justification through the death of the Lord differs significantly in tone from Jesus' proclamation of the kingdom of God. However, recent study has suggested that justification for Paul is to be understood as the coming of God's end-time ('eschatological' as scholars put it) righteousness into the world (rather than just as a doctrine about individuals being put right with God), and so is not so different from Jesus' teaching about the kingdom of God. It is true that Paul uses Jesus' favourite phrase 'the kingdom of God' relatively rarely in his letters (though he does use it occasionally in ways that sound like Jesus, eg 1 Cor 4.20, 6.9,10). It is also true that the concepts of 'righteousness' and 'justification' have a much more prominent place in the letters of Paul (at least in Romans and Galatians) than in the teaching of Jesus. But these differences of terminology are easily explained by the difference of context between Jesus and Paul. Thus 'kingdom of God' was less useful in Paul's Gentile context, and 'justification/righteousness' was a key issue in Paul's debates with the so-called Judaizers.

Divorce

The one point where Paul quite unmistakably picks up the ethics of Jesus is in 1 Corinthians 7, where he cites Jesus' teaching on divorce—as entirely authoritative. Jesus' teaching on divorce is most fully represented in the dialogue with the Pharisees in Mark 10/Matthew 19. In response to their question about circumstances in which divorce may be legitimate, Jesus tells the Pharisees that the Mosaic divorce law of Deuteronomy 24 was to regulate human messiness ('for your hardness of heart') and was not to be taken as divine approval of divorce. God's will, Jesus said, was expressed in the creation narrative of Genesis 2, where God made one woman for one man for life—they are one flesh, and 'what God has put together, let no-one separate.' Jesus goes on to comment that, if separation does occur, then there should be no remarriage, since this is tantamount to adultery. Jesus' teaching is more stringent than that represented in any of the Pharisaic schools, and is seen as shockingly demanding by his disciples, but it is of a piece with Jesus' ethical radicalism. He has announced the coming of the perfect kingdom or rule of God, and in this new situation the old compromises (for example Moses' regulations about divorce or oaths) are no longer appropriate. Now the standard is that of creation.

What does Paul do with this radical teaching of Jesus? The first thing to note is that he knows and cites this teaching . Paul's teaching is quite closely similar to what we find in Matthew/Mark (with first a general injunction not 'to separate' and then a supplementary comment saying that, if there is a separation, the partners should not remarry). The second thing to say is that Paul endorses that radical teaching. In Corinth there were Christians who were advocating an ascetic spirituality, urging those who were married to separate from each other and in particular for those whose partners were unconverted to divorce their partners. Paul, though regarding singleness as an excellent calling, will have none of this advocacy of divorce and total sexual abstinence, citing Jesus' prohibition of divorce as his decisive argument. Paul follows Jesus in referring to the 'one flesh' teaching from the creation story in 1 Corinthians 6.16.[16] Some scholars have thought that Paul (in the case of those married to non-Christians) and Matthew (in the case of those whose partners have been unfaithful) do soften the edge of Jesus' prohibition of divorce slightly; this is not certainly the case. And, even if they do contemplate some exceptions to the rule, they are both quite clear about the rule as such.

---

16 And also by inference in 7.3,4; compare Eph 5.21–33.

Women in Ministry and the Question of Celibacy

If on the matter of divorce Paul seems to be in agreement with Jesus, what about his attitudes to sex in general and to women? Jesus was outstanding for the respect he paid to women—whether to Mary Magdalene, or the woman who anointed his feet, or the Samaritan woman at the well, or Martha's sister Mary, whom Jesus congratulated for sitting at his feet as a listening disciple.[17] But what about Paul? He is often seen as taking a much less liberated line and as arguing strongly that women should take a subordinate position in the church.[18]

At the risk of vastly oversimplifying a contentious issue, we note first the importance of Paul's statement of principle in Galatians 3.28: 'There is neither Jew nor Greek, there is neither slave nor free, there is neither male nor female; for you are all one in Christ Jesus.'[19] Paul here clearly asserts the total equality of all men and women in Christ in a way that is entirely in keeping with Jesus' attitude. That is not to say that Paul would necessarily have assumed that men and women would have the same roles to play in the church (any more than in the family); it is to say that Paul would value women and their part within the body of Christ.

A second observation follows from that. It is clear that Paul greatly valued the ministry of women within the church, and thus he refers appreciatively to women colleagues, notably in Romans 16.

As for 1 Corinthians, one of the letters where Paul seems to have more negative things to say about women's ministry (in chapters 11 and 14), it is worth asking why Paul says these things. The probable answer is that the women in Corinth were acting in an over-liberated manner, thus causing offence! In 1 Corinthians 11 the issue is women praying and prophesying in the church, and flouting convention by doing so with their heads uncovered. An entirely plausible hypothesis is that they did this under the influence of Paul's own teaching—after all he had founded the church just two or three years previously and he had very likely taught then that there should be no distinction between male and female in the church. They were therefore claiming the right to pray and prophesy with head unveiled like the

---

17 We should not exaggerate Jesus' revolutionary radicalism in this matter: as has often been pointed out, he did not appoint women to the twelve, whether for pragmatic or for other reasons; but still women feature in key roles in the story of Jesus, whether it is Mary, Jesus' mother, or the women who visit the tomb.

18 Notably in 1 Cor 11.2–16; 14.33–36; 1 Tim 2.11–15. Some scholars try to rescue Paul from this accusation by denying Paul's authorship of the pastoral epistles and even of 1 Cor 14.33–36; the blame is thus shifted to Paul's unenlightened followers (also in Col 3.18; Eph 5.24). However, it is doubtful if Paul should be rescued in this way, and if he needs it!

19 There is a good case for seeing Galatians as Paul's earliest letter; but, even if it is not, scholars have suggested that Gal 3.28 may be an early baptismal formula (see the context, 3.27).

men.[20] If this is correct, then we see that it was Paul's own continuation of Jesus' radicalism that partially at least gave rise to the problem. But does Paul backtrack on this in 1 Corinthians? No: he approves of the women praying and prophesying (and it is worth remembering how important a gift prophecy is for Paul, see 1 Cor 14). What he objects to is the upset that they have been causing and also what we might call their 'unisex' interpretation of equality in Christ. Paul believes in the equality of men and women, but also in the goodness of creation, including of gender differences; hence his emphasis on the story of Adam and Eve in 1 Corinthians 11.2–16.[21]

A Plausible Reconstruction

One interesting possibility, noted by various scholars, is that it was spiritually liberated women in Corinth who were not only praying and preaching in an uninhibited way, but also advocating sexual abstinence as the way of true spirituality, thus giving rise to the discussion of 1 Corinthians 7 about sex and marriage. If the spiritual women believed, as some of the Corinthians seem to have done, that they were already in the kingdom of God, so much so that they were even speaking with 'the tongues of angels' (1 Cor 13.1), then they might quite logically have inferred that in this new order there should be no marrying and giving in marriage—had not Jesus said as much (Luke 20.35)? Had not Jesus congratulated Mary the spiritual disciple rather than Martha the domestic provider (Luke 10.38–41)? Had not Paul spoken of new creation having come with Jesus, and of there being no male and female—hence arguably no ongoing sexual life? Such a spirituality might also be reflected in other New Testament contexts, for example in 1 Timothy, where some were 'forbidding marriage' (4.3), and where some women were renouncing the bearing of children (which I take to be the background to 2.15, where Paul affirms that salvation and childbearing can go together!).

This reconstruction of what was going on in Corinth is speculative, but plausible. The evidence includes the priority given to women in some of the discussion in 1 Corinthians 7 (for example verse 10) and the possible echoes of the Mary/Martha story (in verses 32–35). Also, if it was 'spiritual' women who were advocating such sexual abstinence, that could help explain why some of the Corinthian men were going to prostitutes (1 Cor 6.12–20). Interestingly the Corinthian men may also have been justifying their actions by appealing to teaching of Paul ('all things are lawful') and of Jesus ('nothing going into a person from outside defiles a person'). What Jesus and Paul said particularly about food, the Corinthians applied to sex, claiming that there was no such thing as bodily defilement. Paul responds to them with a

---

20 Compare 2 Cor 3.14–18 on some of the symbolism of uncovered heads.
21 Compare also 1 Tim 2.13,14.

strong affirmation of the importance of the body. If this reconstruction is correct, then we find not a Paul reneging on the radicalism of Jesus, but Paul discussing its application to the Corinthian situation and following Jesus in affirming the goodness of God's created order—of the body (in response to prostitution), of marriage and sexual relationships (in response to an ascetic spirituality) and of gender differences (in response to a unisex spirituality).

Paul's ethics are thus not a retreat from Jesus, but a continuation of Jesus. This conclusion is confirmed by the way Paul echoes Jesus' ethical teaching in Romans 12–15 and elsewhere, the most conspicuous examples of this being in Romans 12.17–21 (for example 12.17, 'Bless those who persecute you; bless and do not curse'), where there are notable parallels with Jesus' Sermon on the Mount.[22]

Conclusion

The view that Paul's theology is significantly different from that of Jesus must be rejected. At point after point Paul can be shown to be building on Jesus' teaching, not diverging from it.

---

22 Matt 5.38–42; Luke 6.27,33.

3

Does Paul Contradict the Gospels' Story of Jesus?

If there is much more continuity between the teaching of Jesus and that of Paul than is sometimes thought, what about the questions raised by Paul's evidence concerning the major events of Jesus' lifetime as narrated in the gospels, notably his birth and resurrection?

Paul and the Empty Tomb

Arguments about Paul and Jesus' birth are largely arguments from silence, and so it will be best to start with the resurrection, about which Paul does have a considerable amount to say. Indeed Paul is a particularly important witness to the resurrection. 1 Corinthians 15.3–8 is the crucial text. Paul says: 'I passed on to you as of first importance what I also received, that Christ died for our sins according to the Scriptures, and that he was buried and that he was raised on the third day according to the Scriptures, and that he appeared [literally was seen] to Cephas, then to the twelve. Then he appeared to over five hundred brothers at one time, of whom the majority remain until today, but some have fallen asleep. Then he appeared to James, then to all the apostles. Finally of all as to one born out of time he appeared to me.' The importance of this text is that:

a) it is dated with confidence by scholars to AD 54/55 (if not earlier);
b) in speaking of the resurrection as a tradition that he 'received' Paul indicates that it goes back to the time of his conversion in the 30s AD;
c) the list of resurrection appearances may not be part of that earliest tradition, but it is still the earliest account which we have of Jesus' resurrection appearances;
d) it confirms what we saw in 1 Corinthians 11 that Paul's missionary methods included the transmission of traditions of Jesus.

The importance of all this can hardly be exaggerated, but what are we to make of the two questions that are raised by 1 Corinthians for the gospel narratives of Jesus' resurrection?

a) He appears to be completely ignorant of the stories about the women finding the empty tomb, which are primary in all the gospels.
b) He lists himself with the witnesses of the risen Jesus, thus suggesting to many scholars that he sees the resurrection appearances as visionary (like his own).

A number of observations are relevant:

First, Paul's list of the appearances of the risen Jesus appears to be quite deliberately arranged. Thus we have

Cephas/Peter
and the twelve

500 brothers, most of them still alive

James
and all the apostles

It can hardly be accidental: (a) that the two individuals who feature are the two most highly respected leaders of the church, particularly in Jerusalem— Peter the chief apostle, and James the brother of Jesus who became leader of the Jerusalem church (they also, if Galatians and Acts are to be believed, happen to be the church leaders with whom Paul had particular dealings in Jerusalem); (b) that Peter is bracketed with the twelve and James with all the apostles. It looks very much from this as though we have here a list arranged to make a point, and that point is hardly a mystery when we see how Paul goes on in the next verses in 1 Corinthians 15—to refer to his own seeing of the risen Jesus, and to his own 'apostleship.' Paul seems to be making a point about his own apostleship being in continuity with that of the best recognized apostles. Peter has pride of place at the head of the list of witnesses; Paul, though the 'least' of the apostles, has pride of place at the end. The 500 brothers in the middle may not seem to make sense in the scheme. Maybe they are there just because they are so many—it was a startlingly important appearance—but perhaps also to make it clear that it was not just Peter, James, the twelve and the apostles who saw Jesus, but a host of others. If this analysis is anywhere near correct, then it is impossible to deduce much from Paul's failure to mention the women's part in the discovery of the risen Jesus.

Paul's list is schematic and probably selective, and, if Paul knew of women like Mary Magdalene seeing the risen Jesus, he has simply chosen to omit that story. This does not necessarily show anti-feminine prejudice, though the testimony of women would not have carried weight with everyone; it is simply that Paul mentions the two top men—and no one else by name.

Second, it is true that Paul does not mention the empty tomb, but that is hardly surprising, given the nature of Paul's argument. After all, the emptiness of the tomb did not in itself prove the resurrection—the body could have been stolen! However, it is entirely probable that Paul believed the tomb to have been empty. His specific reference to the burial of Jesus followed by a reference to his 'being raised' could hardly have meant anything else to someone like Paul from a Jewish background. Admittedly scholars have tried to argue otherwise, but it is very hard to see how Paul's discussion of the resurrection of the body, both in chapter 6.12–20 and here in chapter 15, could be taken to refer to the survival of the soul rather than to the transformation of the body.[23]

Third, as for Paul's listing of himself with the other witnesses to the resurrection, far from proving that Paul saw the resurrection appearances as visionary like his own, it more probably proves the opposite, namely that he saw his own 'apostolic' seeing of the Lord as a real seeing, not as a vision. The book of Acts suggests that Paul was physically blinded by his 'vision' of the Lord, and it is entirely plausible that Paul thought he had physically seen the Lord—like the other apostles. Indeed, had he understood his own 'seeing' as purely visionary, it is not clear how he could have confidently say 'last of all' about his own vision, since visions of Jesus did not apparently cease in the early church, whereas the resurrection appearances did.[24]

It turns out that the argument that Paul contradicts the gospel accounts of Jesus' resurrection is only an argument from silence, and an unconvincing one at that. The evidence in fact tends to tell in favour of the picture we find in the gospels. Paul confirms the emptiness of the tomb, the chronologically limited timespan when the risen Jesus was seen, and certain of the appearance stories listed in the gospels—notably Luke's account which refers both to Jesus appearing first to Peter on Easter day and to him then appearing to the twelve (Luke 24.33–36).

Paul and the Infancy of Jesus

The situation with the birth of Jesus is less interesting, just because there is so little evidence to go on. But again the argument that Paul is ignorant of the story of Jesus' birth as described by Matthew and Luke is purely an argument from silence. And the silence may not be quite as total as is sometimes thought. The following observations are worth making:

1) Paul refers to Jesus as being 'born of a woman' (Gal 4.4,5), and speaks of God as the Father of Jesus, but nowhere mentions any human father of Jesus.
2) On the few occasions when Paul does speak of the birth and/or origins of Jesus, he expresses ideas that are prominent also in the accounts of

---

23 Compare Phil 3.21.
24 See W Craig, 'The Bodily Resurrection of Jesus,' in *Gospel Perspectives 1*, R T France and D Wenham (eds), (Sheffield: JSOT, 1980) pp 47–74. Even if that argument is not decisive, much cannot be made of Paul's listing himself with the other witnesses of the risen Jesus, since Paul specifically notes that he was in a special category.

Jesus' infancy in Matthew and Luke—thus he speaks of Jesus coming in the fullness of time (Gal 4.4),[25] of Jesus as descended from David (Rom 1.3),[26] and of Jesus as born under the law (Gal 4.4).[27]

3) When Paul refers to the birth and/or origins of Jesus, he avoids the usual word for 'being born' (Greek *gennaomai*), though he uses this of the birth of other people (for example Abraham's children in Gal 4.21–31). When speaking of Jesus, he consistently uses the verb *ginomai*, which means broadly 'become.'[28] It is quite possible that Paul deliberately avoids the word *gennaomai*, which in its active form refers to the male act of begetting a child (as in Matthew 1 of the ancestors of Jesus).[29]

These observations do not add up to proof that Paul knew the story of Jesus' miraculous birth as described in the gospels, but they are certainly compatible with that view. The argument that Paul is a witness against the gospel story, though repeated very recently indeed by so distinguished a scholar as John Macquarrie, carries no weight at all.[30]

Conclusion

The view that Paul puts a big question mark against important gospel stories is unpersuasive: he does not say a lot directly, except about the Lord's death and resurrection, but what he does say supports rather than contradicts the gospel narratives.[31]

25 Compare Matt 1 and especially the hymns of Luke 1 and 2, for example the Magnificat, Benedictus and Nunc Dimittis.

26 Compare Matt 1.17,20,21; 2.5,6; Luke 1.32,69; 2.4,11.

27 Compare Jesus being presented in the temple in fulfilment of the law in Luke 2.22–24.

28 Rom 1.3; Gal 4.4; Phil 2.7.

29 C E B Cranfield, 'Some Reflections on the Subject of the Virgin Birth,' in *Scottish Journal of Theology* 41 (1988) pp 177–98.

30 In the pre-Christmas edition of the *Church Times*, 19 December 1997.

31 Paul refers directly to hardly any of the events of Jesus' pre-passion lifetime, but there are all sorts of hints which may point to his familiarity with the stories: we have mentioned the story of Jesus' baptism; he may also have known the story of the transfiguration (note for example his references to the glory of God in the face of Jesus and to Christians being 'transfigured' in 2 Cor 3.18; 4.6), and the story of Jesus sending out the twelve with authority (there are many echoes of the mission discourse in 1 Cor 9, including 9.14, as mentioned before, and Paul refers to the 'signs of an apostle' in 2 Cor 12.12).

4
How Much Did the Jesus Tradition Matter to Paul?

Finally we come to the general question of Paul's interest or lack of interest in the stories and sayings of Jesus. His failure to refer explicitly and directly to these traditions indicates to some scholars that Paul and no doubt others in the earliest church were not very interested in the history of Jesus. But that view underestimates the weight of indirect evidence of Paul's dependence on the traditions of Jesus. Some of this evidence has been noted already, and there is much more.

Further Evidence from Galatians and 1 and 2 Thessalonians
For example, in Galatians 1 and 2 Paul writes to defend his apostleship in dialogue with people who were questioning it and comparing him unfavourably with the proper and original apostles like Peter. Paul insists that his apostolic ministry to the Gentiles is comparable to Peter's to the Jews (Gal 2.8). What is clear in his discussion is that he is familiar with the tradition of Peter's primacy among the apostles, and he very likely knows of a tradition that Peter was commissioned specially by Jesus (see Matt 16.16–20). There is no way of proving what commissioning story he knew, and yet it is intriguing how in describing his own apostolic call in Galatians 1.11–17 he uses language that has striking similarities to Matthew 16.16–20. In this gospel passage Peter, after his confession of Jesus as Christ and Son of God, is congratulated by Jesus on his insight: 'Blessed are you, Simon bar-Jona, for flesh and blood has not revealed this to you, but my Father in heaven…' Paul speaks of his own calling in somewhat similar terms, referring to God's gracious revelation of his 'Son,' to his experience of 'revelation' and to the non-involvement of 'flesh and blood.' The verbal and conceptual parallels by themselves would not prove anything, but the context of Paul comparing himself with Peter, and the fact that Paul presupposes the Lord's commissioning of Peter, encourage us to think that Paul is deliberately portraying his commissioning as parallel to that of Peter.

Paul's reference to Peter as apostle to the circumcised and elsewhere to Jesus as 'servant of the circumcised' (Rom 15.8) make it also quite feasible that Paul was familiar with the traditions recorded, again in Matthew's gospel, of Jesus sending the twelve on mission specifically to the Jews and of Jesus describing his own mission as 'to the lost sheep of the house of Israel' (Matt 10.5, 15.24). Paul, though proud of his calling as apostle to the Gentiles, is quite open about the saving work of God in Christ being 'first to the Jew, then to the Greek' (Rom 1.16).

Even more important evidence is in 1 Thessalonians 4 and 5, where Paul speaks about the second coming of Christ in ways that are unmistakably reminiscent of the teachings of Jesus in, for example, Matthew 24 and 25. The clearest example of this is probably the reference to the day of the Lord coming 'like a thief in the night' (1 Thess 5.2), which has widely been recognized as an allusion to Jesus' parable about the Lord coming unexpectedly like a thief.[32] But there are many other possible links between Paul's teaching and that of Jesus in the synoptics. Paul's reference to Jesus coming with a trumpet call has a parallel in 'the trumpet shall sound' in Matthew 24.31 and his discussion of 'those who have fallen asleep' responding to a cry of command and rising 'to meet' the Lord may well be connected with Matthew's parable of the wise and foolish virgins (Matt 25.1–13). Paul's description of the Lord coming suddenly and inescapably on the complacent like labour pains on a pregnant woman may well be connected with Luke's ending of Jesus' 'eschatological discourse,' where Jesus warns of his unexpected coming and counsels prayer that 'you may be able to escape' (Luke 21.34–36).[33]

The parallels are considerable, though often not given much attention by scholars. But do the parallels prove that Paul was dependent on the teaching of Jesus? We noted before the dangers of 'parallelomania,' and of seeing significance where the similarity may simply be coincidence. Even if it is not coincidence, may it not be that the parallels noted reflect the fact that Paul and the synoptics are drawing on common Jewish traditions about the endtime, rather than Paul's dependence on Jesus? Or, if there is indeed a relationship between the synoptic teaching and Paul's, are we sure that Paul is dependent on Jesus, rather than Paul being an influence on the synoptic evangelists? These are important questions, and lead us to pause to comment briefly on what is an appropriate and sound method in addressing the issue.[34]

Method in Assessing Parallels Between Paul and Jesus—Some Detective Work!

Essentially our task, when we seek to assess the parallels between Paul and Jesus, is to be a good detective—not credulous, but seeing whether the different pieces of evidence add up to a strong case. We must certainly be open to the possibilities of coincidence and/or common Jewish background (certainly the trumpet at the end-time could be so explained), and we must

---

32 A so-called 'Q' parable, found in Matt 24.42–44, Luke 12.39–40.

33 The list of possible connections between Paul's eschatological teaching and that of Jesus could be expanded, especially if we were to include in our purview 1 Thess 2.14–16 (with its intriguing similarity to Matt 23.33–36/Luke 11.47–51, also Luke 21.23,24) and 2 Thess 2 (if this is rightly seen as Pauline), where the description of the coming of the man of lawlessness is very similar to the synoptic gospels' description of the desolating sacrilege (Matt 24, Mark 13, Luke 21).

34 This has been most helpfully and fully discussed by Michael Thompson in his *Clothed with Christ* (Sheffield: JSOT, 1991).

consider whether Paul influenced the synoptic evangelists. However, if the parallels of wording are particularly striking, then this makes coincidence less likely; if the parallels are substantial and not just verbal, then this too diminishes the likelihood of coincidence. If there is no particularly obvious Jewish background (as with the thief in the night image), then this makes a connection between the New Testament traditions more likely. If there are specific indications in Paul's teaching that he is referring back to an earlier tradition, then this supports the view that the direction of dependence is from Jesus to Paul and not *vice versa*.

A good example of such an indication is in 1 Corinthians 7.10, where Paul specifically says that the teaching he is presenting on divorce is from 'the Lord'; when that attribution goes along with evidence from the gospels ascribing just such teaching to Jesus, it is hard to avoid the conclusion that Paul is dependent on Jesus. There are not many such clear cut indications,[35] but in the teaching about the end-time of 1 Thessalonians 4 Paul can refer to a 'word of the Lord' on the fate of Christians who have died (4.15). This is plausibly seen as an indication that Paul is drawing on a tradition here, and, despite the doubts of some scholars,[36] the probability is that this 'word' is some of Jesus' teaching about the end-time (including perhaps the parable of the virgins), which is so strikingly similar to Paul's own teaching.

Assessing the probability of dependence will involve a careful weighing of the evidence in each case. Sometimes the verdict may be 'unlikely,' sometimes 'possible,' sometimes 'probable.' But, although each case must be weighed, there is also an important cumulative ingredient in the whole argument. One particular parallel may by itself be very uncertain evidence for Paul's dependence on Jesus-traditions, but in the context of other less ambiguous evidence the balance of probability may begin to tip in favour of dependence. Thus in 1 Thessalonians 4 and 5 the 'thief' is strong evidence for Paul's dependence on Jesus, (a) because of the testimony of Matthew and Luke (or 'Q') to the tradition originating from Jesus, (b) because the idea has no Jewish background, and (c) because no one other than Jesus within the Christian movement is likely to have compared Jesus to a thief (not even Paul!). If the 'thief' is Jesus' word, then this lends weight to the hypothesis that 'the word of the Lord' of 4.15 is indeed Jesus-tradition, and also suggests that others of the possible echoes of Jesus in the context deserve to be upgraded from 'possible' to 'probable.'

The cumulative argument is not only important within the specific context of the teaching on the end-time in 1 and 2 Thessalonians; it has much wider relevance. There is a small, but very significant, quantity of what we

---

35 1 Cor 9.14; 11.23 are others.
36 Some have surmised that Paul is drawing on a Christian prophecy.

might call 'hard' evidence for Paul's familiarity with and use of Jesus-traditions. The hardest evidence is in 1 Corinthians (with the divorce saying, the reference to the labourer being worthy of his hire, the last supper traditions, the resurrection traditions), but then there is also good evidence in 1 Thessalonians, as we have seen; Romans is not far behind, notably with the ethical teaching of chapters 12–15; and there is less sure evidence from Galatians. All of this put together adds up significantly, and other 'possible' evidence in those letters and elsewhere in Paul's writings comes to look 'probable'; for example, it seems likely that Paul's comment about being 'persuaded and convinced in the Lord Jesus that nothing is unclean in itself' in Romans 14.14 is an allusion to the saying of Jesus in Mark 7.15 about nothing from outside defiling a person. Paul agrees with Mark's interpretation of that saying as 'cleansing all food,' but not with the Corinthians' interpretation of the same saying as justifying immorality.

Why is Paul Not More Overt in Referring to Jesus?

Although in this booklet we have only been able to mention briefly some of the evidence for Paul's familiarity with the Jesus tradition, it should have become clear that there is a strong case for thinking that Paul was familiar with, and influenced by, a great many traditions about Jesus. I have argued that case much more fully in my full-length treatment of the subject *Paul: Follower of Jesus or Founder of Christianity?*

But, if that case is to stand, we must say something more about Paul's failure to refer directly to the stories and sayings of Jesus. It is all very well detecting echoes of Jesus all over Paul's letters, but why are there only echoes and not more direct references? Does not this after all show that Paul is not very interested in the historical Jesus, even if he has been influenced by traditions about him? If the story of Jesus before his passion was really of interest and importance to Paul, would we not expect to see and hear more of it?

This is a serious objection to the position we have been proposing (and has been made by reviewers of my book). A number of points are relevant in response to the objection.

First, the sheer quantity of echoes and allusions to the stories and sayings of Jesus that we have identified makes it clear that traditions of Jesus were extremely influential in the earliest days of the church. Even if they are not owned as Jesus-traditions explicitly by Paul they have permeated his teaching to an extent that indicates their importance in the early church.

Second, the failure of Paul explicitly to identify the Jesus-traditions he uses as coming from Jesus could possibly be because he did not know that they were such, but is more probably because they were extremely well-known, indeed foundational to Paul and to his readers. If they were well-known and foundational, two consequences might follow: (1) Paul might sometimes echo Jesus intentionally and expect his readers to pick up the echo without him drawing their attention to it; (2) he might sometimes echo Jesus just because Jesus' teaching had become built into his own thinking, without intending to make any point that it originated from Jesus.

Third, there is very important evidence showing that Paul did pass on traditions of Jesus to his converts, notably in 1 Corinthians 11 and 15, where Paul reminds the Corinthians of how he had taught them about the last supper and resurrection. Here is hard evidence that Paul did pass on stories such as we find in the gospels.[37]

Fourth, what is particularly important to note about those passages from 1 Corinthians is that Paul highlights those Jesus-traditions because the Corinthians had particular problems—with the Lord's supper and over the resurrection of the dead. That is a very significant observation for a consideration of Paul's 'silence' regarding things to do with Jesus, because, had the Corinthians not had those particular problems, Paul would not have written about them, and we would have had no inkling whatever that Paul knew anything about the Lord's supper (no inkling indeed that Paul's church had eucharistic meals), and no inkling that Paul knew anything specific about the resurrection appearances. Rather similarly, had the Corinthians not had problems in the area of sex, we would have had no evidence that Paul knew the teaching of Jesus on divorce.

The importance of this evidence can hardly be exaggerated in response to those who make much of Paul's silence about other things in Jesus' ministry. The point may be put this way. If we had all the Pauline letters except 1 Corinthians, we would have no clear evidence of Paul's knowledge of the Lord's supper, the resurrection appearances and of Jesus' teaching on divorce. We might well conclude from his silence that he was ignorant of them, or uninterested in them. But we would be very wrong indeed. So we should not conclude from his silence about other things that he was ignorant or uninterested, and indeed we should take the hint provided by all the indirect evidence that there is and conclude the opposite, namely that a wide range of Jesus traditions were taught by Paul to his churches.

Fifth, although the case for interpreting Paul's 'silence' in this way is strong, it is also true, as we have suggested, that for Paul writing after the death and resurrection of Jesus those events were of primary importance to him, putting other things about Jesus into the shade. Paul's teaching does have a different focus and emphasis from that of Jesus himself, because he is writing after those events, and after the coming of the Holy Spirit, and in the context of a missionary church working among Gentiles. This new context gives his

---

37 The traditions in question concern the passion not Jesus' pre-passion ministry. But there is no reason whatever to suppose that the story of Jesus effectively started for Paul 'on the night when he was betrayed.'

21

teaching a different focus from the pre-passion teaching of Jesus, but it does not mean that the pre-passion teaching and ministry of Jesus have ceased to have importance for him. The evidence is that Paul and his churches are familiar with the whole story of Jesus, that they discussed and debated it, and that it was indeed part of the foundation that was regularly laid by Paul when establishing churches.

The Gospel that Paul Preached

This surely makes sense—that the preaching and teaching of the Christian gospel in Paul's and other churches regularly included a narrating of the story of Jesus. Scholars sometimes seem to suppose that the preaching of Jesus comprised only the sort of pithy statements that we find in verses like 1 Corinthians 15.3,4 'Christ died for our sins according to the Scriptures, he was buried, he was raised the third day.' But these verses are patently only summary statements, and it is totally improbable that either preachers or their hearers will have been satisfied with such 30-second explanations of the truth that is in Jesus! People will have wanted to know what happened before the night that Jesus was betrayed (as well as to know more of what was being referred to in the phrase 'according to the Scriptures').

What will they have been told? The most concrete evidence we have of how the story of Jesus was narrated in the early church is in the gospels themselves. The question is: did such gospel narratives go back to the time of Paul? We cannot prove that, but two things can be said. First, the traditions that we find in the gospels must have been being passed on in some form in the time of Paul. Second, Paul specifically refers to having passed on gospel-like traditions of Jesus. Some critics tell us that in the earliest period of the church's life the stories and sayings of Jesus were passed on piecemeal within the general teaching of the church about Christian living, not specifically as traditions of Jesus that were to be preserved. But the evidence of Paul tells against this view: he does not use the stories and sayings of Jesus incidentally in his letters in such a way that a future evangelist would later be able to make a gospel out of them, but he does refer to passing on stories of Jesus.

The conclusion that Paul's churches will have been taught many of our gospel stories makes sense in view of what we have said about the quantity of echoes and allusions. Furthermore, although you could hardly even begin to write a gospel on the basis of what Paul says about Jesus, it is interesting to see how, given a prior knowledge of the gospels, we can recognize fragments of the story they tell at various points: we have noted Galatians 4.4 'God sent forth his Son born of a woman born under the law' and its similarity to the infancy stories of Luke in particular. Romans 1.3,4 is also particularly interesting. Paul here speaks of 'the gospel of God'—and then he goes on to describe that gospel as follows:

'The gospel of God

1) which he promised beforehand through his prophets in the holy scriptures,
2) the gospel concerning
   his Son,
   a) who was descended from David according to the flesh
   b) was declared Son of God with power according to the spirit of holiness
   by resurrection from the dead,
   Jesus Christ our Lord,
3) through whom we have received grace and apostleship to bring about
   the obedience of faith among all the Gentiles for the sake of his name.'

The interesting thing about this description of the gospel from our point of view is how very similar it is in form to our written gospels, notably to that of Matthew. Matthew starts (1) with the Old Testament (with the genealogy of Jesus). He then proceeds (2) with the story of Jesus from his birth to his resurrection, and ends (3) with the commissioning of the disciples to go to all the nations.

We have seen how Paul was familiar with many parts of the story of Jesus as attested in the gospels, and, although some scholars may hardly dare to imagine this, it is entirely conceivable that Paul knew not just individual traditions of Jesus, but an extended account of Jesus' life and teaching, which we would recognize as similar in form to our gospels.

This possibility must become a probability if Luke the companion of Paul was the author of Luke's gospel. The evidence for this is good. Not only is the early church clear that he was, but the internal evidence in the book of Acts points in this direction, particularly the 'we' passages of the book of Acts (20.6ff). Although scholars have tried to offer other explanations of this use of the first person, easily the most likely explanation is that the author of Acts (and hence of Luke's gospel) is indicating his presence with Paul at these points in the narrative.[38]

If the author of Luke's gospel was the companion of Paul, then the importance of the stories and sayings of Jesus for some of those who worked with Paul is quite clear, and we may guess with some confidence that Paul (Luke's hero in Acts) and Luke would have had a common interest in those traditions. It is probably no accident that at a number of points Paul seems to represent Luke's form of the gospel tradition rather than that found in Matthew and Mark (for example in the account of the Lord's supper).

---

38 The remarkable topographical accuracy of these sections of Acts strengthens the case for Lukan authorship (and is in no way nullified by the supposed divergence between the Paul of Acts and the Paul of the Pauline letters).

Conclusions on Paul and the Historical Jesus

If even most of the argument I have presented is well-founded, then Paul turns out not to be at odds with the historical Jesus, not to undermine the gospel stories, not to show the unimportance of the historical Jesus. In fact, Paul turns out to be a most important witness to the historical Jesus. He attests very many of the gospel traditions, albeit obliquely most of the time, and he shows that the story of Jesus was foundational (not irrelevant) to the earliest church, and carefully transmitted.[39]

What is the importance of these conclusions? They are clearly important for the reader and interpreter of Paul's letters, since, if those letters presuppose the stories and sayings of Jesus, they need to be read in that light. They are building on what we find in the gospels, even if the gospels were not actually in written form at this time. They are also very important for the historian wanting to know about Jesus and the early Christian movement, since Paul testifies to Jesus (directly or indirectly), and also shows us how the stories and sayings were used, debated and interpreted in the earliest days of the church. Finally, they are important for the Christian wishing to commend Jesus to others and facing difficult questions about Paul. Paul turns out to be a strong ally, a help not a hindrance, because he turns out to be a faithful follower and apostle of Jesus Christ, whose writings lend strong and very early support to the story of Jesus that we know from the gospels.[40]

Further reading

V P Furnish, *Jesus according to Paul* (Cambridge: CUP, 1993), a simple introduction to the subject, seeing a less close connection between Jesus and Paul than I see.

A J M Wedderburn (ed), *Paul and Jesus* (Sheffield: JSOT, 1989), a collection of scholarly essays from different points of view.

M Thompson, *Clothed with Christ* (Sheffield: JSOT, 1991), an important and detailed discussion of Romans 12–15 and of the question of method, taking a similar position to my *Paul: Follower of Jesus or Founder of Christianity?* (Grand Rapids: Eerdmans, 1995).

---

39 He also throws interesting light on the 'synoptic problem' (the question of the relationship between Matthew, Mark and Luke), because he attests not only Lukan traditions (Luke's form of the last supper, the story of Mary and Martha, etc), but also so-called 'Q' traditions (like the thief in the night), and also traditions only found in Matthew (the commissioning of Peter, the limitation of Jesus' mission to the Jews, the parable of the wise and foolish virgins, etc). Paul may even attest distinctive traditions of the fourth gospel: for example, when in Gal 6.2 Paul urges the Galatian Christians to 'bear one another's burdens, and so fulfil the *law of Christ*,' it is very possible that he has in mind Jesus' so-called 'new commandment' to his disciples that they should 'love one another,' to which the fourth gospel alone refers (13.34; 15.12,17). The potential importance of this conclusion can hardly be underestimated: if Paul, writing in the 40s and 50s, attests what scholars have called Markan, Q, M, L and Johannine traditions, then this is an excitingly significant factor to take into account in assessing the history of gospel traditions.

40 It is not an unfortunate accident that so much of the New Testament relates to the life and writings of Paul—rather the opposite!

St. Roger of Beel

by

Stephen P. Nunn

Published by

Maldon Archaeological and Historical Group

Registered Charity - No. 285387

2001

This book is dedicated in loving memory of
my late father, Peter Nunn.

ISBN   0 9511948 4 4

Publication funded by
Maldon Archaeological and Historical Group

CONTENTS

ACKNOWLEDGEMENTS

During the course of this research I have been very fortunate in receiving assistance from a number of individuals and organisations. My thanks go out to them all but in particular I would like to record my appreciation for the help that I have had from: Mrs. Earnshaw and the late Mrs. Shacklock at Thomas Plume's Library, Maldon, for pointing me in the direction of seventeenth century works on Roger. My friend, the local historian and current Librarian of Thomas Plume's Library, Dr. W.J. Petchey, and Mr. Alec Taylor, of King Edward VI Grammar School Chelmsford, for the translation of Latin texts. Jane Ringrose, Medieval expert, and D.J.Hall, Deputy Librarian of Cambridge University Library; Dr. Nick Barratt, Reader Services Department, and Paul Johnson, Image Library Manager of the Public Record Office; Mr. J. Wisdom, Librarian, St. Paul's Cathedral Library; The Librarian of the British Library; Father Anthony Marrett-Crosby, OSB, of Ampleforth Abbey, North Yorkshire; and C. Hugh Lawrence, Emeritus Professor of Medieval History at the University of London; for their help with primary source material. The staff of the Essex Record Office and the staff of Chelmsford Library (Local Studies Collection), for their help with later, secondary source material and printed books - a select bibliography is included at the end of this publication. H. Joy Tait for correcting typescript.

I would also like to acknowledge the encouragement given to me during the course of my research by the following; the late June Prime of Maldon Society; Ecclesiastical authors Trefor Jones and Joseph Gribben; the late Christina Foyle and W.R.Christopher Foyle of Beeleigh Abbey; Rt. Rev. Thomas McMahon, Bishop of Brentwood; Robert S. Taylor of Wycliffe Hall, Barnard Castle; The Prior of the Canons Regular of Prémontré (Storrington); Michael Shrewsbury and Pat Farquar, Prebendaries of St. Paul's; Sister Gabriel, Ursuline Sisters (Brentwood); Jim and Joan Green; Les and Ann Puttock; Chris Danes. I am also extremely grateful to the committee and members of the Maldon Archaeological and Historical Group for publishing this work - particularly the co-ordinating skills of the Chairman, Derek Punchard, and the preparation work by Ken Cook.

Above all I would like to record my love and deep appreciation to my wife, Christine and our daughter, Catherine, for tolerating my regular absences from family life whilst I travelled back to the thirteenth century via the word processor!

INTRODUCTION

Go into any High Street book shop or public library, look at any one of the many 'Dictionaries of Saints' and it is very unlikely that you will find reference to a Saint Roger - well at least not a Saint Roger Niger de Biliye. Then turn to any of the countless histories of medieval England and the chances are that the only 'Niger' you will find, will be the completely unrelated theologian and chronicler, Ralph Niger. Circumstances have meant that Saint Roger's story is a largely untold and forgotten one. Even his feast day, the 29th. September, clashes with Michaelmas, the better known feast of Saint Michael.

Until his death in 1241, and throughout succeeding centuries up to the Dissolution of the Monasteries, Saint Roger was a principal character in the history of the English Church. He enjoyed something of a comeback at the hands of seventeenth century antiquarians, slipped into the shadows again, and then re-emerged during the 1920s. This brief revival in the 1920s occurred when the historian J.H. Round, a significant figure in our search, wrote a paper about the Saint. This inspired further research and even the production of two plays, but by the late 1930s the Saint's name had again returned to obscurity.

In his research, Round highlighted an association between Roger and Beeleigh, in Essex, commenting that even the Saint's surname seemed to incorporate the place-name. Beeleigh, an East Saxon name meaning 'clearing in the trees where bees are kept', is still a fascinating place. It lies on the outskirts of the parish of St. Peter's, Maldon and is now a small rural hamlet occupied by a handful of people, living in just a few surviving buildings. This is a picture far removed from past glory. Pottery fragments indicate that the place has been settled since Bronze Age times. A water mill operated here from the Domesday era until it was destroyed by fire in 1875. Similarly a windmill once stood on a piece of high ground, sometimes inaccurately referred to as a tumulus or burial mound. Beeleigh has evolved over many centuries and since Victorian times has enjoyed considerable patronage from tourists, writers and artists - not least Sir Edwin Landseer. Above all this however, the jewel in the hamlet's crown must be Beeleigh Abbey and it was here that Roger's ecclesiastical career was said to have started and to a certain extent where it apparently came to an end.

The Saint's story is revealed as one of humble beginnings and of a gradual but determined climb through the ranks of the established church. It centres on a turbulent period of English history, the late twelfth and thirteenth centuries, and is a chronicle of political intrigue, of matters spiritual and secular, of power, wonder and eventual "canonisation". It is also a tale of archaeological mystery, conjecture and romanticism. But more than anything else this is a search for an all but unheard of Saint with local, Essex associations, Roger Niger, almost Maldon's patron saint.

Stephen P. Nunn
Maldon, Essex

84   DE EPISCOPIS

XLIV. ROGERUS NIGER.

Rogerus Niger. (s) Euftachii loco à Canonicis electus eft è gremio fuo Rogerus cognomento *Niger*, in Catalogo Paulino *Le Veir* dictus (*Le Non* effe legendum opinor) *S. Rogerus de Byleis* dicitur ab Adamo Murimuthenfi. *Rogerus Niger de Bileye* in libro Statutorum antiquo MS. in Bibliothecâ Publicâ Academiæ Cantabrigienfis : Quæ quidem Statuta ipfe compofuit, & Rectoribus ac Sacerdotibus Archidiaconatûs Londinenfis præfcripfit (ff). *Vir in literaturâ profundâ pectoris, honeftus à per omnia laudabilis ; religionis amator ac defenfor, omni genere fuperbiæ carens, vitæ venerabilis, & miræ fanctitatis, fcientiâ præclarus & prædicatione perfpicuus,*&c. Confecratus (t) eft apud Cantuariam ab Henrico Roffenfi Epifcopo 1229. Junii 10. unà cum Ricardo Archiepifcopo & Hugone Elienfi. A Jocelino Bathonienfi Epifcopo confecratum fuiffe tradunt Annales Waverleienfes ; qui eundem Archidiaconum Colceftriæ antea fuiffe teftantur. Archidiaconum quidem Colce-

LONDINENSIBUS. 85

ftriæ fuiffe confirmant Annales vetufti MSS. Cœnobii Mertonenfis. Affluebat hoc tempore Anglia Italis mercatoribus utriufque Ordinis. Ecclefiaftici Beneficia Ecclefiaftica in Angliâ adepti, redditibus eorum in Italiam afportatis Anglos expoliârunt. Sæculares, qui Caurfini dicebantur, indultâ à Pontifice veniâ, Anglos, ac præfertim Religiofos, ufuris miferè depauperârunt. (u) Primorum horrea populares tumultu facto diripuerunt Anno 1232. Direptores Rogerus anathemate percuffit : iifdem tamen clanculùm faviffe infimulatus, Romam adire coactus eft, ut fe purgaret ; nec fine gravi pecuniæ mulctâ à Papa dimiffus rediit. Caurfinos Rogerus Anno 1235. excommunicavit. (v) Hi autem nummis in Curiâ Romanâ effufis tantum Epifcopo negotii faceffebant ; ut fententiam revocare & perditiffimis expilatoribus fræna laxare neceffe haberet. Nec minore fortitudine Rogerus adversùs Regios miniftros libertatem Ecclefiafticam violantes decertavit. (x) Hubertum de Burgo, Comitem Cantiæ, qui ex fummâ potentiâ delapfus, Regem fibi infenfiffimum expertus eft, fatellites Regii ex Capellâ quâdam in Diocefi

(r) Paris, p. 353, 363, &c.   (t) Annales MSS. ab 1066.
(ff) Paris, loc. cit.   ad 1321.
ftriæ

(u) Paris, p. 418.   (x) Idem, p. 329.
(v) Paris, p. 418.

G 3   Londinenfi

Roger enjoyed something of a comeback at the hands of seventeenth century antiquarians. This is a section from H. Wharton's 'Historia' of 1695. (Reproduced by permission of the Trustees of Thomas Plume's Library, Maldon).

1. THE FOUNDATION OF BEELEIGH ABBEY AND ROGER'S BIRTH.

Towards the close of the twelfth century a community of White Canons moved from their Abbey at "Perhendune", or Parndon, (a region now occupied by Harlow New Town), to a site within the hamlet of Beeleigh, granted to them by the then Lord of the Manor of Little Maldon, Robert Mantell. Beeleigh Abbey, originally simply known as the Abbey of Maldon (Beeleigh not occurring in the name until the following century), existed from 1180 until its eventual suppression under the Act of Dissolution in 1536. The White Canons in question belonged to the Order of Prémontré, which had established itself in this country in 1143. Parndon, and in turn Beeleigh, were colonised from New House in Lincolnshire, the first abbey of the order in England.

At about the same time that the Premonstratensians migrated to Maldon, a baby boy was born to a couple named Ralph and Margery. They christened their child Roger, a name which the later, seventeenth century poet Michael Drayton thought to be entirely appropriate, for he refers to the Christian name in song twenty-four of his mighty work 'Poly-Olbion' (first published 1612 and 1622) and associates its origin with an ancient word for "rest", "repose" or "quietness", saying:

> "Thus Roger hath a roome in this our sainted throng
> Who by his words and workes, so taught the way to Heaven
> As that great name to him, sure vainely was not given"

In contemporary, medieval documents Roger is referred to variously as Roger "Niger", "le Noir", "le Meyr", "le Vier" or simply "The Blacke"; "de Biliye" or "de Byleie".

The early surname "Niger" (le Meyr and le Vier being clerical mistakes) refers as a rule to the complexion of skin or to the colour of hair. "Blacke" is a Middle-English spelling of Black whilst "Niger" is Norman or "Old-English". However, Roger had a younger brother, Walter, Canon of St. Paul's and one time Vicar of Navestock near Ongar, who is also recorded as "Niger". This would appear to indicate that both inherited an existing family surname from their father and that it did not necessarily describe their own appearance.

"De Biliye", on the other hand, is what is known as a "locative by-name", denoting, according to an excepted practice of the time, that Roger Black was literally "of Beeleigh"- in other words he was a native of that place. Although very little is known of his early life, this gives us our first tangible clue to an association between Roger and Beeleigh and it could well be that Ralph and Margery presented their son to God and to the newly founded Abbey for the religious life. If this was the case, then the Canons may have supervised his education and prepared him for a career in the Church. A notable example of this type of child oblation is Saint Bede, who was offered to the Abbot of Monkwearmouth, County Durham, at the age of seven to be educated. Junior entrants to monastic houses would have worn a variant of the habit, would have acted as choristers and acolytes and usually pursued a religious profession when they reached canonical age. However, the practice of child oblation was in fact dying out after the middle of the twelfth century and Roger's name could be simply "toponymic" – that is associated with the hamlet rather than the Abbey.

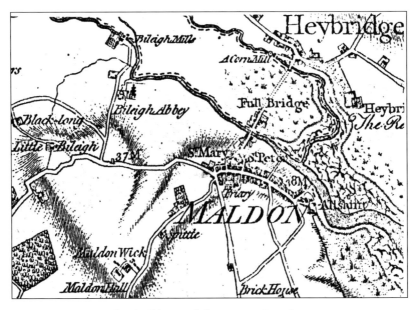

Beeleigh Abbey and the surrounding district.
From the Chapman and André survey of 1777.

Later dissolution records certainly reveal that Beeleigh Abbey had a "Children's Chamber", an indication that it could well have been a place of tuition. How many boarders were there at any given time is unclear. There was only one bed in the chamber by 1536, but as a modern-day historian has reminded us "until the early nineteenth century, children usually slept several to one bed"! Did Roger start his education here? Did he sleep in a forerunner to that humble chamber? Did he have Robert and Henry, the first two Abbots, to thank for early patronage? We may never know the true answers to these tantalising questions, but there is no doubt that Beeleigh had a special meaning for Roger. It featured in his surname and although we must now move away from the place to reveal the rest of his story, ultimately, we will need to return to discover the final episode in Roger's mortal existence.

2. A TILLINGHAM PREBEND

The next we hear of Roger (and it is, indeed, the first date that can be verified by primary documentary sources) is in 1192, by which time he appears to have left Beeleigh to follow an ecclesiastical career and is in residence at St. Paul's, in London, where he is mentioned as a "prebendary of Ealdland".

A "prebendary" is a Canon who is a holder of a "prebend". A "prebend" is, in turn, revenue from an estate owned by the cathedral and granted to the Canon as a stipend. In Roger's case his allowance was drawn from a property or tithe called 'Ealdland'.

Although the place-name is no longer used, it was originally an area within the parish of Tillingham on the Dengie marshes. The Dean and Chapter of St. Paul's had been Lords of the Manor of Tillingham as early as 610, possessing large tracts of land in the area, including Hall Farm, 'Thrushes', 'Blackbirds' and 'Reculver Land'. 'Ealdland', simply meaning 'old land', implied that even by 1192 it had been long under cultivation.

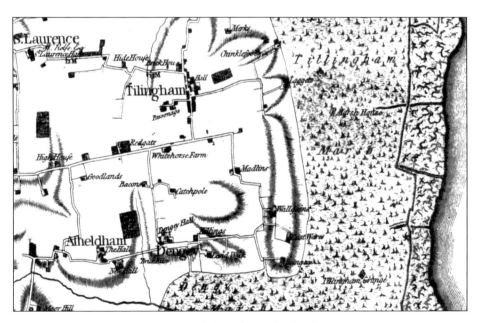

Farmlands around the village of Tillingham, Essex
From the Chapman and André survey of 1777.

10

The first recorded prebendary of Ealdland was one 'Quintilian', who was appointed in 1103. It then passed to his son 'Cyprian', and so on, through seven separate holders (including Laurence, the nephew of Pope Celestine III) until John de London vacated it in preference of Roger Niger in 1192. With the prebend came a seat in St. Paul's Cathedral - in fact it was the tenth Stall on the left of the Choir - and a requirement that Roger should recite, on a daily basis, the 82nd. to the 86th. Psalms inclusive, from "God standeth in the congregation of the mighty ......" to "Bow down thine ear, O Lord, hear me: for I am poor and needy ....". The 83rd. Psalm includes a very poignant line, which would become relevant to a crucial event in his later life and one which many would believe endorsed his importance within the Christian church:

"...... As the fire burneth a wood, and as the flame setteth the mountains on fire;
    So persecute them with thy tempest, and make them afraid with thy storm".

The Ealdland Prebendary survives to this day. It still includes a seat in Wren's St. Paul's Cathedral and continues to involve the recitation of the same Psalms - some 800 years after Roger's term of office. The corps, or endowment of Ealdland would have provided Roger with a comfortable enough income to complete any studies possibly begun at Beeleigh Abbey, thus allowing him sufficient qualification to consider his next career move within the established church of the time, but even he could not envisage what truly great things lay ahead.

3. ARCHDEACON OF COLCHESTER

In 1218 Roger occurs as Archdeacon of Colchester. This Archdeaconry also had its administrative base at St. Paul's and a corresponding seat within the Cathedral - this time it was the last Stall on the right side of the Choir. Similarly, a prebend was attached to the appointment at one time drawn from income generated by the church at Ardleigh, near Manningtree (Roger was involved in giving consent to this arrangement) although indications are that he continued to receive the Ealdland income whilst Archdeacon. In reality, Roger would have rarely left St. Paul's, conducting most of his business from there. To enable this to happen he occupied a group of houses on the south side of the churchyard - a property he latter assigned to his successors.

As Archdeacon, Roger's jurisdiction incorporated six Deaneries; Newport which contained twenty parishes; Sampford, consisting of twenty-two; Tendering, thirty-four; Lexden, forty-three; Colchester itself containing sixteen parishes and Witham, with twenty-three, including the churches at Goldhanger, Langford, Great and Little Totham, Ulting and the important ecclesiastical seat of Wickham Bishops, location of an ancient moated house belonging to the Bishops of London - from which the parish name is derived.

Surviving grants, licences and charters illustrate some of Roger's activities during this period and give us "snapshots" of his work as Archdeacon. It was an office of considerable importance with full jurisdiction, including the right of visitation, administration of church property and responsibility to conduct ecclesiastical courts. He appears on a Licence granted to Richard, Abbot of Waltham, to build a chapel in the parish of St. Mary-Hill London. He was a witness, with others, to the Deeds of some mills at Wapping in 1218 and to some land in Aldbury, Hertfordshire, in 1219. A charter made between William, Abbot of St Albans and Robert de Watford, the Dean, in 1221 also bears his name; as does an ordination of the vicarage of Witham in 1222. He witnessed the restoration of rent from property in St. Ouen, France (no doubt associated with the abbey there) to St. Paul's, circa 1226, and further revenue from the churches at Bumpstead and Finchingfield , circa 1228, to be granted to the "poor clerks and choir of St. Paul's".

He also issued a collection of statutes for the rectors and priests of the Archdeaconry and, incredibly enough, this document (albeit a slightly later copy) survives to this day and is preserved in the Cambridge University Library. It consists of sixty-nine separate paragraphs, each containing regulations for the conduct of the clergy on procedures in a variety of situations, such as burials of excommunicates and the duties towards the Chapter of St. Paul's Cathedral. It begins: "Statuta inter rettores Archidiaconi London' per d'inum Rogerum bone memorie Nigerum de Bileye quondam London' episcop' edicta et constituta......", which translated means: "The Statutes announced and enacted for the rectors of the Archdeaconry of London by Master Roger, of good memory, the Black of Beeleigh (and) Bishop of London". The statutes end with a note in a later hand indicating that this manuscript copy of the original statutes was completed on the tenth of November 1317.

Tantalising elements, not least addressing Roger as of "good memory" – equivalent to "the late Roger" - and calling him one-time "Bishop of London", lead us towards much more important developments as we shall now see.

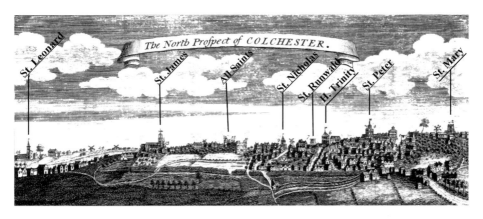

A prospect of Colchester showing some
of the churches under Roger's control.
From Philip Morant's 'History of Colchester' (1738).

The opening page from the collection of Statutes for the Rectors and Priests of the Archdeaconry of Roger Niger. He is recorded as "Master Roger of good memory, the Black of Beeleigh".
(Reproduced by permission of the Syndics of Cambridge University Library.)

4. BISHOP OF LONDON

Eustace (sometimes termed Eustachius) de Fauconberge, Bishop of London, died on the 31st. October 1228 and the Dean and Chapter of St. Paul's chose Roger as his successor. He was formally elected in 1228 and his elevation to the See of London was confirmed by his Consecration on Trinity Sunday, the 10th June, 1229. The ceremony took place at Canterbury and was conducted by Henry Sandford, Bishop of Rochester, Richard de Wethershed, Archbishop of Canterbury and Hugh Northwold Bishop of Ely. He was the forty-first occupant of the position and, according to his contemporary, the St. Alban's monk and writer/historian, Matthew Paris, a perfect choice for he was:

> "….a very reverend man, religious, learned, painful in preaching, eloquent, a great house-keeper, of very gentle and courteous behaviour ....".

We may again obtain some idea of his work as Bishop by turning to surviving manuscripts and there are many which contain references to Roger. During his first year of office he was involved in confirming earlier charters and grants associated with the liberties of St. Paul's, giving licence to build a chapel in Hertfordshire and confirming the sale of land in Middlesex and the grant of a manor in Acton, also in that county, to St. Paul's.

The following year (1230) he gave the church of Little Henham to the priory and canons of Little Dunmow and instituted a vicarage there. In 1231 he was party to an agreement which transferred some jurisdiction of Kilburn Priory, London, from Westminster Abbey to St. Paul's, became involved in a dispute about the ownership of Ware, Middlesex and bore witness to a grant by Pope Gregory IX to his Dean and Chapter.

The period 1236/37 was a particularly busy one for Roger with; a dispute between St. Paul's and the Abbot and Convent of Walden (1236); the receipt of Takeley vicarage from the Abbot of Colchester (1237); problems with the jurisdiction of Barkeway, Middlesex; the grant of certain churches in Essex and Hertfordshire to the Abbot of St John's, Colchester and in turn from St. John's to St. Paul's of other Essex churches and confirmations associated with a "chapel of the Park", in Lexden and 'Manor Chapel', Brightlingsea.

He instituted one Gilbert to the church of Elsenham, Essex, in 1238, and other numerous, but largely undated issues incorporate his name, including; a problem with the rights of patronage at Heydon, near Royston; a dispute with Westminster Abbey over the Chapel of St. Leonard, in Foster Lane, London and a similar event connected with Northall vicarage.

Interesting as these are, they are really no more than the routine work and responsibilities of an albeit powerful and influential medieval Bishop. Roger was, however, involved in much more than that and it is to these extraordinary events that we must now turn.

St. Paul's Cathedral and the Thames.
From a panorama by J.C.Visscher (1616)

5. A TEMPEST OF THUNDER AND LIGHTNING

A bishop's responsibilities were (and indeed still are) many and varied and as well as the secular and administrative tasks already discussed, Roger was of course a principal character in the spiritual life of the bishopric, taking an obvious lead in prayer and regular service. On the 25th. January, 1230, an important date in itself for it was the anniversary of the Conversion of St. Paul, Roger was involved in one such service, high mass within his cathedral.

There then came, in the words of Matthew Paris (reproduced by many subsequent historians, not least John Weever in his 'Ancient Funeral Monuments' of 1631) "a sudden darkness (which) overshadowed the choir and therewith came such a tempest of thunder and lightning that the people there assembled thought verily the church and steeple had come down upon their heads". If this was not frightening enough there then followed,….. "such a filthy savor and stink that partly for fear that they might not abide the savor, they voided the church, falling on heaps one on another as they sought to get out of the same".

Even the vicars and canons forsook their desks but despite the terror and chaos that ensued, Bishop Roger was unmoved and assisted by one remaining deacon that served him at mass, he calmly finished the service. Afterwards when the air began to clear up the people returned into the church and were humbled by what they saw; the bishop who, as it was recorded "remansit intrepidus".

Lightning was seen at the time as some kind of divine vengeance. One mid-thirteenth century account reporting on similar weather conditions says that; "the Lord thundered horribly and terrifyingly…..and a sudden flash of lightning struck…..the sin-avenging flame flew like a fire-breathing dragon…..". Roger must have thought that the words within the 83rd. Psalm, so well known to him from his Ealdland prebend days, were about to come horribly true. It must have appeared to him that his cathedral was going to be destroyed by "fire" and that his congregation would be "persecuted by tempest" and "made afraid by storm".

Despite this, his faith obviously allowed him to remain firm and there is no doubt that this event would have a major bearing on his future earthly, but perhaps more importantly, his heavenly status.

6. HUBERT DE BURGH

The social and political picture of the reign of King Henry III is both a colourful and a complex one. Henry inherited a kingdom that was still coming to terms with defeats on the Continent and with the implications of Magna Carta (we will hear more about the Carta and an association with Roger later). Whilst still a minor and until 1232, Henry reigned under the regency of a succession of powerful justiciars, or heads of government - William Marshal, Peter des Roches, and Hubert de Burgh. There was constant conflict within his court by the insular Anglo-Norman nobility at the appointment of "foreigners" to high offices in government and further difficulties in relations with the papacy and the Church. It was within this setting that a crisis of state developed, and in the words of one historian, it was Roger Niger who defused it by "reconciling enemies and excommunicating the obdurate".

Peter des Roches, the Bishop of Winchester, was a controversial figure. Seen as one of the most powerful "foreigners" at court he was a natural life-long rival of Hubert de Burgh, the Earl of Kent who upheld the right of Englishmen to all offices. The rivalry reached its peak when in 1232 des Roches accused de Burgh of treason. The King was convinced and Hubert fled for his life. He initially went to Merton Priory, in Surrey, but then made for Bury St. Edmunds in the hope that he would join his new wife there. On his way he was intercepted at Brentwood - then known as 'Boisars' - by a force said to consist of 300 soldiers.

His nephew, the Bishop of Norwich owned a house there, but he sought sanctuary in a small, wayside chapel the ruins of which can still be seen in Brentwood High Street. The chapel was founded in 1221 by the monks of St. Osyth as an ancillary to South Weald church and was used by pilgrims on their way to the shrine of St. Thomas Becket at Canterbury - hence the corresponding dedication to St. Thomas. In the thirteenth century, when the power of the Church was at its height ecclesiastical privileges were jealously guarded and the establishment of a chapel was not a matter of course, needing at the very least the consent of the incumbent and patron of the parish church and of the bishop. Within the chapel Hubert de Burgh; "held the cross of Our Lord in one hand and the body (Sacrament) of Our Lord Christ in the other", claiming his legal right of sanctuary for the statutory forty days. This did not stop the soldiers however, who seized him at the altar and took him to be imprisoned in the Tower of London.

The St. Alban's chronicler, Roger de Wendover, says that a local smith was called for to fetter his feet, but he would have nothing to do with the job. Upon hearing the news Roger, in a courageous move, threatened to excommunicate the King, his officers and all those concerned for their violence and wrong doing against the holy church.

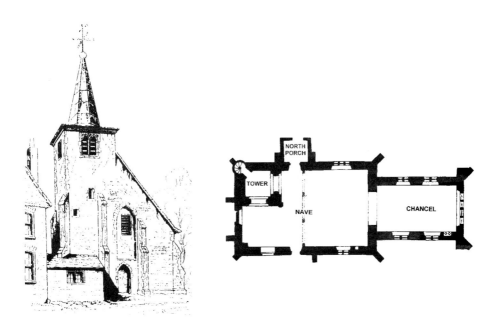

The chapel of St. Thomas, Brentwood.
(From G. Buckler's "Essex Churches", 1856)

Whether it was through fear of excommunication (Henry III was considered a very religious monarch) his knowledge of Roger whom he had consulted at Oxford in June of the previous year on the affairs of Wales, or a conscience towards his former friend and confidant de Burgh, we shall never know, but he relented. Hubert was returned to the "place from whence he was fetcht" - the chapel of St. Thomas Becket at Brentwood. Notwithstanding this, his private seal was "ground to powder" and a strong watch was kept on the chapel by the sheriffs of Hertford and Essex. Although initially allowed a halfpenny loaf and a large measure of beer a day, an order was made not to communicate or procure anything for him. A ditch was dug around the chapel and de Burgh was finally starved into surrender after thirty-nine days.

Roger had, however, given the King time to cool down and had bought de Burgh enough time to prove his innocence. Despite the protestations of des Roches he was, after a further incident and representations by Roger, Pope Gregory IX and others, later pardoned and his rights and privileges restored, but he lived the rest of his life in retirement (he had a house at Clavering) and away from the position of public power that he had previously enjoyed. Roger, on the other hand, had demonstrated that he was a force to be reckoned with and he would hence forth be listened to and be actively involved in other matters of government and state.

7. THE ROAD TO ROME

In the same year as the de Burgh affair (1232), Roger actually exercised his power to excommunicate, on this occasion against a group of people who had been guilty of violence towards Roman clerks (in particular an incident that occurred at Wingham in Kent and another involving one of the canons of his own cathedral). This occurred during the time of a popular movement against the growing practice of providing "foreign", papal nominees to benefices in England. Hubert de Burgh was alleged to have been a prime protagonist as was Robert Tweng, a young Yorkshire landowner, who won considerable support at the king's court as well as in the countryside.

Notwithstanding Roger's apparent hard line, he was himself accused of consenting to the pillage of Romans and summoned to the Pope. In reality Bishop Roger had been in conflict with Rustandus, the Pope's diplomatic representative, or nuncio, who had been collecting moneys to send abroad to his master. This action, along with Roger's previous open support for de Burgh, resulted in the Pope's displeasure and associated instruction.

Roger duly obeyed and made his way to Rome, stopping for a short time at Parma, now in Northern Italy, but formerly the capital of a Duchy of the same name. Whilst there, and to make matters worse, he was robbed of his jewels and money. Although he was able to recover a portion with some difficulty, the event would feature heavily in a future, bloody encounter, for in 1247 the city was besieged by Frederick II.

Emperor Frederick II, the "Wonder of the World", self-styled "King of Jerusalem" and scourge of the Pope, made war on various Italian towns and blockaded the people of Parma for three solid months for daring to shift their allegiance from him to the pontiff. The citizens, according to Matthew Paris, declared; "We deserve these sufferings for.....ours is the city in which that holy bishop of London, Roger.....was cruelly robbed of the necessaries for his journey and other valuables and (was) never paid compensation when he was travelling to the papal curia. When he left next day, he placed a curse on this city and its inhabitants". When Parma was eventually liberated, the people, relieved and apparently in praise and thanks to God, "........took the trouble to find out how much money the bishop claimed to have lost and .... (decided to) make satisfaction .... either by building a church in London or in the giving of alms...".

That did not assist Roger at the time, of course, and already removed of money by way of the cost of the journey and the robbery, he was forced by the Pope to purge himself further and at great expense for his alleged wrongdoing against Rome. He returned to England in the Autumn of 1233, a poorer, wiser but as we will discover from subsequent events concerning yet further excommunication and money issues partly associated with Rome, a possibly more determined man.

A seventeenth century map of Italy

8. WALTER MAUCLERK

Roger's return to England was via Dover, the important Cinque Port dominated by the strategically placed castle whose constable was, until his earlier downfall in 1232, none other than Hubert de Burgh. As Roger stepped ashore he literally walked straight into yet another potentially international crisis.

Walter Mauclerk Bishop of Carlisle and one-time treasurer of the exchequer had just been expelled from his office to make way for Robert Passelow and through the influence, yet again, of Peter des Roches. Additionally he was fined one hundred pounds, a substantial amount by anybody's reckoning. Mauclerk, determined to appeal to the Pope, attempted to board a ship and make for Rome. He was, however, "violently stopped" and arrested at Dover by the King's officers on the pretext that he did not have the monarch's permission, leave or licence to "go beyond sea" and depart the realm.

The Cinque Port of Dover, dominated by the Castle.
From a view by Samuel and Nathaniel Buck (1735)

Hearing of this and unabashed by his previous experiences, Bishop Roger at once excommunicated the officers and went to the King at Hereford, where he remonstrated with him for having ordered the arrest. In the King's presence and, apparently without fear for himself or any resulting consequences, he once again renewed the excommunication.

Following the removal of de Burgh, Mauclerk was the only remaining "link with the past" at court and des Roches was keen to see the back of him. The King, however, listened to Roger, Mauclerk was released, allowed to go to Flanders, eventually pardoned and soon recovered the Royal favour.

One can imagine a semi-satisfied Roger Niger having, almost at the eleventh hour so to speak, exercised his influence again over Henry III. He had won another victory against the "foreigner", his old adversary, des Roches, had resurrected his right of excommunication but as we shall now see, he was ready to address an even more important concern - money.

9. TAXATION AND EXCLUSION

The monetary dispute between Roger and Rustandus, the Pope's nuncio or diplomat in this country, that indirectly resulted in the Bishop's summons to Rome, illustrates only too well the pressures associated with thirteenth century ecclesiastical financing. Roger and other Anglo-Norman sympathisers were keen to ensure the collection of dues to fund local foundations - from the mighty St. Paul's Cathedral to the smallest parish church. As such, any removal of moneys by "foreigners" or papal representatives did not match this aim.

In an attempt to address both of these important issues, Bishop Roger took action at two key levels:

Firstly, and to ensure local church funding was adequate, he introduced a major financial constitution. He ordained that all the citizens of London should pay their parish priests one half-penny in the pound out of their earnings, and a farthing out of every ten shillings every Lord's Day, and also every Festival whose Vigils were to be observed as Fasts. This decision proved to be so successful if not popular with the ratepayers, that it was subsequently confirmed by Thomas Arundel,

A silver penny of Henry III. (Author's collection).

Archbishop of Canterbury, in 1397, and ironically enough, by a succession of Popes including, Innocent VII, in 1404, Nicholas V, in 1453, and via a Bull of Pope Nicholas, which the Common Council of London adopted on the 3rd. March 1464, some 230 years after Roger's initial action.

Secondly, whilst Roger must have appreciated from his previous experiences that direct intervention over the collection of income by the papacy would only result in another summons to Rome, he nevertheless looked, as a separate issue, at ways of dealing with this difficult problem within his own diocese. Usury, the distasteful practice of lending money with very high rates of interest was largely performed by the Caursines.

The Caursines, or 'Caorsins', were originally inhabitants of Cahors, in Languedoc, an infamous seat of Italian money-changers and financiers throughout the Middle Ages. Commonly mentioned along with Lombards and Jews, Matthew Paris says that they: "Found a place of refuge and peace in

England. First tolerated and then openly protected by the Pope, they called themselves merchants or money changers of the Pope.....".

With this protection they carried out their business in London, extracting high stakes from the citizens, with a percentage no doubt, finding its way to Rome. In 1235 Roger acted and endeavoured to expel all of the Caursines from his area of jurisdiction. They, in turn, used their influence with the papal see and procured, once again, Roger's summons to Rome.

This must have been a great disappointment for Roger Niger and unable through ill health to obey, he was compelled to yield. Just five years later, however, the Caursines were expelled from England by Henry III, readmitted on the intervention of the Pope in 1250 and again proscribed and imprisoned "on account of their unbounded and detestable usury" in 1251 - perhaps Roger was right after all?

10. AFFAIRS OF CHURCH AND STATE

As well as overarching financial concerns, Roger was actively involved at this stage of his life in a variety of matters associated with church and state. He officiated, for example, at the consecration of Edmund as Archbishop elect of Canterbury, on Laetare Sunday, the 2nd April 1234. An illustration of the event survives in the Historia Anglorum by Matthew Paris, both Edmund and Roger being represented in the drawing. Edmund of Abingdon (later Saint Edmund) was elected to Canterbury both in the presence of the King and at the insistence of Pope Gregory IX. Despite this papal support, Archbishop Edmund emerged as the champion of the national church against the claims of Rome and the leader of the Barons and Bishops in a successful campaign to have Peter des Roches finally removed from office. Edmund's relationship with Roger, however, appears to have been a fairly stormy one, for in 1239 they entered into a bitter quarrel over the rights of Episcopal Visitation. A Bishop's right to examine the state of his Diocese by way of an official tour or inspection was believed to be relatively sacrosanct and the dispute seems to have been around Edmund's claim to visit religious houses in the Diocese of London.

We also hear of Roger taking part in the coronation of the Queen, Eleanor of Provence, in January 1236 at Westminster Abbey, and assisting at the baptism of her son, the future King

The Consecration of Archbishop Edmund of Canterbury by Roger Niger, Bishop of London,(right). Drawn by Matthew Paris in the margin of the Historia Anglorum. (Reproduced by permission of the British Library. Royal MS 14c vii).

Edward I in 1239. Roger was actively involved in obtaining the release of one Radulf le Breton, a canon of St. Paul's, whom the king had imprisoned. Additionally Roger was a witness to the re-issue of Magna Carta.

The Carta, or Great Charter of Liberties, was first issued by King John in 1215. It was generally regarded as the fundamental statement of English rights, but was really the product of a rebellion. John was a distrusted monarch and was forced into a programme of reform which was drawn up in the form of the Charter. After John's death in 1216, the supporters of his son, Henry III, re-issued a modified charter. They did so again in 1217 and in 1225, when it entered the statute books.

When in 1236, rumour spread that Henry III was trying to repudiate his obligations to observe certain elements of the Charter, he was forced into renewing it and to support the church in sentences of excommunication against anyone who dared to infringe the principles. According to the Dictionary of National Biography, Roger was a witness to this re-issue of the Charter "in 1236". The correct date was, however, the 28th January and is listed against the year 1237. The document still survives in the Public Record Office and is under the regnal year of 21 Henry III - which extends its proper form as 1236/7 - and it maybe from this reference that the confusion over the existence of a 1236 re-issue originates.

Despite the dispute over dates, contained within the list of witnesses to the re-issue is a reference to "R Lond" which was the standard scribal formula for the Bishop of London. The 'R' stands for the Bishop's Christian name, in this case a reference to our very own Roger Niger.

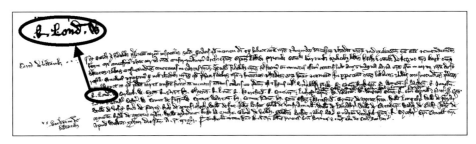

The 1237 re-issue of Magna Carta.
"R.Lond" appears as a witness - extreme left, sixth line from the top.
Reproduced by permission of the Public Record Office)

11. ST. PAUL'S CATHEDRAL

Throughout his ecclesiastical career, Roger had very close associations with St. Paul's Cathedral. This relationship existed as early as his prebendary days, during his time as an Archdeacon and was reinforced following his appointment as Bishop of' London in 1229. He was keen to exercise good works and to ensure the upkeep and development of the place. He gave large sums of money towards this aim and his episcopate was marked by much progress in the building. In the words of the seventeenth century antiquarian, Sir William Dugdale: "That this Roger was a great benefactor to the......fabrick, cannot be doubted ......".

As early as 1229-30, Bishop Roger;   ".....confirmed whatsoever Maurice, his predecessor, had granted thereto towards St. Paul's and moreover ratified all those oblations, made at Whitsuntide, which Eustace de Fauconbrigge (the immediate foregoing bishop) had restored for the same purpose.....".

Roger also founded a chantry at St. Paul's for the souls of his late parents, Ralph and Margery. A chantry was an endowment for the signing of masses for the deceased. Most chantry masses were said by chantry priests at side altars and, at a later stage, such altars were located within specially constructed chantry chapels.

The nave of old St. Paul's Cathedral as illustrated in Sir W. Dugdale's 'History' of 1658. (Reproduced by permission of the Dean and Chapter of St. Paul's)

The St. Paul's that Roger knew is, of course, now long gone as it was tragically destroyed during the Great Fire of London in 1666. Even that Cathedral was not the earliest to have occupied the site. According to the Dark-Age scholar/monk, Bede, the first Cathedral was founded in 604 by Saint Ethelbert King of Kent. This building was razed to the ground by fire and rebuilt in stone between 675 and 685 by Eorconweald, the 4th Bishop of London - more of him (or at least his mortal remains) later. This, the second St. Paul's, was destroyed by the Vikings in 961. The third, Saxon Cathedral was also lost to fire in 1087. The construction of the Norman Cathedral began immediately afterwards under Maurice (the Bishop of London already mentioned in the 1229-30 confirmation). Built of Caen stone, "Old St. Paul's" became one of the largest buildings in England, topped by the tallest spire ever to have been built. At the west end were two great bell towers and at the east a beautiful rose window.

Work undertaken during Roger's incumbency reached its culmination with the dedication of a new choir. The previous choir, although well proportioned to the eastern body of the church and cross aisles, was felt to be too plain. Roger had the architecture "perfected and beautified" and completed the project in time for consecration on the 1st. October, 1240. In attendance was King Henry III; Edmund, Archbishop of Canterbury; Otto, the Pope's legate, or representative; six other Bishops; many nobles and magnates; and, of course, Bishop Roger himself.

The occasion was felt to be so important that Roger procured, "...an indulgence of forty days pardon (or forgiveness) to all those (people who were there and) .... agreed to truly confess of their sins". The indulgence was to, "...stand good also on the anniversary of the said dedication for ever".

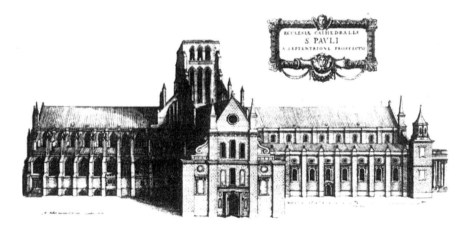

Old St. Paul's. From a view by Hollar (1656).
The spire had already been destroyed by lightning in 1561.

How must Roger have felt on that solemn Autumn day all those years ago? The occasion obviously marked an important achievement in the development of the Cathedral and a major personal accomplishment by Roger. Equally it must have felt like a watershed in his career, for all of those distinguished persons present represented important chapters in his past life, the stormy relationships with the monarchy, Canterbury and Rome, issues of power and money, of "foreigners" and "nationals", and so much more besides, but what of the future - what did that hold?

12. DEATH AND BURIAL

Just twelve months after the completion of his work at St. Paul's, Roger Niger died. He departed this life on Michaelmas Day, 29th. September, 1241, at Bishop's Hall, in the parish of "Stupenheath", or Stepney. This manor had been possessed by the Bishops of London since 1000 (and remained theirs up to the reign of Edward VI) and it appears that Roger retired to that place with failing health. Immediate public reaction to his passing appears to have gone largely unrecorded, but events "post-mortem" would change all of that.

The body of Bishop Roger Niger de Beeleigh was taken to St. Paul's Cathedral where it was buried, "at the ninth hour within the quinzaine of Michaelmas" - in other words, at three o'clock in the afternoon and within fifteen days of the date of his death. At that precise moment and to the astonishment of those present an eclipse of the sun occurred.

It is difficult to say where his first tomb was located as records seem to indicate that it was, perhaps on more than one occasion, subsequently moved. In about 1319-20, for instance, the body of Saint Eorconweald (the early Bishop of London mentioned in the previous chapter) was, "in the night time to avoid too great a confluence of people, removed to the chapel (of the Blessed Virgin) and solemnly placed there in the new shrine, as was also, within eight days after that Roger de Byleie (Niger), from the place where it lay to another prepared for it.....".

What is clear, however, is that Roger's last resting place - that is prior to the Great Fire of 1666 - was between the north aisle and the beautiful choir that had been so special to him during his life on earth. The actual location is described variously as, "in the enter close, or north wall of the presbytery, a little above the quire", "in the north aisle, near the choir", "near to the preaching place in Saint Paul's Church" and "in the midst of the quire, near unto the preaching place", but Dugdale, in his 1658 'History of St. Paul's' gives us detailed and most importantly, first-hand bearings: "Standing between the fifth and sixth pillars (reckoning from the west) of the choir and touching the fifth pillar".

An engraving of this ultimate tomb is also given in Dugdale's work, together with four lines of verse and a prose epitaph that were apparently inscribed on it. The tomb was of grey marble and looked very much like the original one associated with Saint Thomas, at Canterbury - strong walls, a large slab on top and arched apertures in the side wall through which pilgrims could place their hands, heads, or in some cases whole bodies, to be closer to the coffin.

Translated from the Latin, the associated verse read: "Here lies buried, in the year one thousand, two hundred, and forty (sic), Roger, formerly president of the present church. By his hands this place was dedicated to the Lord. O Christ, by his prayers grant pardon to take away (our) offences".

Roger's tomb in St. Paul's Cathedral prior to the Great Fire of 1666. From Sir W. Dugdale's 'History' of 1658. (Reproduced by permission of the Dean and Chapter of St. Paul's).

An associated tablet over, on, or hanging next to the tomb, read (again after translation) as follows: "Here rests in the Lord Roger, surnamed Black, once canon of this church of St. Paul and then consecrated into the bishopric in London in the year of our salvation 1228. A man deep in literature, honourable in character, and throughout everything a praiseworthy lover and energetic defender of the Christian religion. He, when he had directed his pastoral duty wakefully and enthusiastically for fourteen years, closed his last day at his manor of Stepenheath on 29th. September in the year of Christ 1241, while King Henry III was reigning. It happened in these days, while that Bishop Roger was standing in this church before the greater altar wearing priestly gear to celebrate the divine (offices), that so great a thickness of clouds occurred in the air that one man could scarcely make out another. (There)

33

rapidly followed this a terrible shaking of thunder, with so great a flash of lightning and unbearable stench that all who were present, rapidly fleeing, expected nothing more certain than death: the bishop alone with one deacon remained fearless. When the air had at last cleared, the bishop completed the remainder of the divine business".

This appears to be a later inscription - perhaps associated with the early fourteenth century re-internment - but wherever the original tomb was located, it was immediately seen as a "special place". As early as the 26th. April 1242, the King, although Roger had often withstood him face to face, allowed, "a wax candle to burn before the body in St. Paul's" and remitted an earlier fine of ten marks. Shortly after this date, things allegedly began to happen in the area of Roger's resting-place.

> **Ecclesiæ quondam Præsul præsentis, in anno**
> **M. bis C. quater X. jacet hic ROGERUS humatus:**
> **Hujus erat manibus Domino locus iste dicatus;**
> **Christe suis precibus veniam des, tolle reatus.**

The four lines of verse from Roger's tomb
(After Sir W. Dugdale, 1658).

13. SAINT ROGER

Matthew Paris tells us variously that "many miracles were wrought at the tomb of Roger" that there were "wonderful events" and that the place "shone forth with remarkable (happenings)". Although these "wonderful events" remain unspecified, people were clearly feeling that in death as well as in life, Roger was a special figure.

Then, in 1249, Roger is referred to in a manuscript as "sanctus" – "Saint Roger". By the thirteenth century canonisation was a solemn judgement reserved by canon law to the pope. By this date we have copious records of the canonisation process in every case, including the records of commissions of inquiry and the ultimate proclamation of the admission of a new candidate to the calendar of the saints that appear in the papal registers of letters. We also have records of a number of causes that were promoted from England unsuccessfully (e.g. those of Robert Grosseteste, the Bishop of Lincoln, and Robert Winchelsey, Archbishop of Canterbury). Roger's canonisation was never formally requested from the Holy See and he was possibly one of the number of high medieval bishops for whom a popular local cult was established. There are other similar examples, like that of Robert of Abingdon (Saint Edmund's clerical brother), and Simon de Montfort who was the object of a popular cult for a few years after his death in 1265.

Roger's "saintly status" ensured a constant stream of pilgrims, determined to see the tomb, to pray, to hope for a miracle and to leave their dues. In 1252, Hugh de Northwold, Bishop of Ely, granted an indulgence (a remission of temporal punishment due for sins) of thirty days to all who visited the tomb of "beatus Rogerus episcopus et confessor". A similar allowance was made in the same year by Richard, Bishop of Exeter, and in the following year by Laurence, Bishop of Rochester. John le Breton, Bishop of Hereford, made his grant in 1269 and at least eleven other separate privileges followed. "Obits'", or memorial services, were also observed in the name of Saint Roger and his "shrine" became a major attraction, yielding substantial income for the Cathedral.

As well as the burial site, "relics" of Saints also inspired the medieval faithful, giving them a sense of power and mystery. It was truly believed that a Saint was simultaneously in Heaven and in their earthly remains, or in things associated with them during their lifetime. Items connected with Roger became all important. St. Paul's Cathedral also held a "Pulvinar magnum.....quod fuit episcopi Rogeri", or large cushion which once belonged to Roger. A "Capa S. Rogeri episcopi, de rubeo sameto, breudata cum stellis et rosis" - Roger's ecclesiastical cope (a cloak or cape) of red, with a hood and with stars and roses on it and made of a rich dress-fabric of silk, interwoven with gold, called Samite, was also preciously preserved at the Cathedral.

Other relics were cared for at locations away from St. Paul's. At the alien priory of St. Melaine, Hatfield Regis, or Broadoak, Essex, for example, a large, gold episcopal ring, which once belonged to "St. Roger of Byleye" was jealously guarded. The ring would have been one of Roger's insignia of office when Bishop of London and it was left to the priory in the will of Alicia, wife of John de Bledlawe of Hatfield Regis, in 1311. The document also provided a cow as a "foredrove" (an animal to be driven before a corpse at a funeral) and bequeathed money and payments to the monks of St. Melaine and to the vicar and chaplain of the parish. Above all, however, she left the special ring "to be kept with other relics in the convent church".

Another, much more unusual object also found its way to Saint Roger's native abbey, the little Premonstratensian foundation at Beeleigh, on the banks of the River Chelmer, near Maldon.

Hatfield Regis Priory.
Roger's Episcopal ring was kept here.
(Essex Review XLIV).

14. RETURN TO BEELEIGH ABBEY

As recently as 1923, the distinguished historian John Horace Round wrote a paper for the 'Transactions of the Essex Archaeological Society', entitled 'The Heart of St. Roger'. In it he referred to a recently published work, also compiled by the Archaeological Society, containing reprints of medieval 'Feet of Fines for Essex'. A Fine, or Finis/Finalis Concordia, was a legally binding document which put a "final end" to all suits. Three copies of each Fine were originally made and one of them called the "Foot" was retained among the records of the Court. The Essex "Feet" were reproduced by the Society in 1910 and Round was particularly interested in entry number 1044, in volume one, listed under 33 Henry III, that is during the regnal year 1248-49.

The Fine in question went to the assizes during "Michaelmas term", which until 1641, began on the 9th or 10th October, and ended on the 28th or 29th November. In it John, the Abbot of Maldon, the plaintiff agreed to hold, "One virgate of land (usually about thirty acres) with appurtenances in Little Meudone.....in pure and perpetual alms, free and quit from all secular service and exaction" from the Lord of the Manor, William de Fanecurt and Roesia, his wife. (Roesia was in fact the granddaughter of Robert Mantell, the founder of Beeleigh Abbey). In return the Abbot agreed that he, and his successors would, ".....find and maintain one cereum (or wax-candle) to burn (on behalf of the de Fanecurts) every day at the Mass of the Blessed Virgin Mary and at the great Mass of the high altar in the church of Meudon before the heart of St. Roger for ever.....".

John Round used this scant piece of evidence to demonstrate the incredible truth that Saint Roger's heart had been removed before his interment in St. Paul's and had been sent to his native Beeleigh Abbey as a Holy Relic! The historian then went on to give examples of other "heart burials", including; Richard (Coeur de Lion), who was slain in the south of France in 1199 and whose heart was buried at the capital of his Duchy in Rouen; King John who died in 1216 and had his heart sent to Croxton Abbey, whilst his body went to Worcester Cathedral and Randulf, the Earl of Chester, who died in 1232 and whose body was buried in Chester, whilst his heart was cared for by the White Monks at their Abbey of Dieulacres, Staffordshire, and so on.

In all fourteen examples were given spanning the twelfth to the seventeenth centuries. Many others could have been quoted, but apart from the above sample, two, in particular, could be seen as having direct relevance to the Saint Roger remain. Richard Poore, Bishop of Chichester, Salisbury and then Durham, died in 1232, had his body interred at Chichester and heart at Tarrant Dorset "where he was born". The un-named wife of Gilbert Peche, patron of Barnwell Priory, Cambridge, had her heart "encased in lead and placed before the high altar". Archaeological evidence of such a lead container has been revealed amongst the ruins of St. Augustine's Abbey in Canterbury, Kent where a large ashlar, containing a cylinder of lead, complete with tight fitting lid has been excavated.

A medieval depiction of a Saint's Shrine

The 1923 paper created great interest at the time and resulted in extended correspondence in the Transactions, a dedicated section on Saint Roger in Fowler, Clapharn and Galpin's excellent history of Beeleigh Abbey and even the production of two plays – Episode III in the '750th Anniversary Drama' of 1930 and another entitled 'St. Roger his Ring' (1934), both of which were performed several times at the Abbey. The Beeleigh entry in volume two of the earlier 'Victoria History of the County of Essex' (1907) provides us with another clue as it states that "Pope Boniface IX, on 22nd July, 1391, granted relaxation of six years and six quadragene (the forty days of Lent) to penitents who on the feast of St. Roger (29th. September) should visit (Beeleigh) and give alms to the church of the monastery". This particular pope was always generous to English saints during his pontificate, in part at least because of the support given to him by English bishops during the great Schism, but the grant of an indulgence to this cult is remarkable precisely because it does not come with any formal canonisation.

The picture then is one of a saintly heart, perhaps sealed in lead and taken to the Abbey in a ceremony of great solemnity by the Deacons of St. Paul's, London, sometime between September 1241 and the Autumn of 1249. For its own security and for its greater glory, it was no doubt housed in a shrine, or richly guilded and decorated casket. Many pilgrims, both great and lowly, would have visited the place and donated the obligatory gifts. These would have generated a considerable income for the Abbey and it is hard to believe the strongly held proposition that "religious houses did not accept the care of a relic without some remuneration".

If the burning of many cereum (or wax-candles) is any indication of the attention given to the heart then an entry in the Maldon Borough Chamberlain's Accounts for 1516 could be particularly telling: "for work on Fulbridge, the town bought from the.....Abbot of Bileighe.....wax". The wax would have been from the gutterings of hundreds, maybe thousands, of candles and possibly used by the Borough as a paste to prevent the wood of the bridge from rotting.

The Abbey became so important a place during the late thirteenth century that a Royal visit occurred in 1289. King Edward I returned from France in the August of that year, landing at Dover. He then made visits of devotion to the shrines of many saints, starting with that of St. Thomas Becket at Canterbury. He then stayed at Leeds Castle, in Kent, and Rayleigh Castle, in Essex. From Rayleigh he went to Bicknacre (or Woodham Ferris) Priory and so on to Beeleigh. He arrived on the 9th September and was joined by his Queen, Eleanor of Castile, on the 10th when masses were celebrated in the abbey (no doubt before the high altar and, therefore, Saint Roger's shrine) for the soul of Hugh Fitz Otho, the King's steward, who had been a benefactor to the house. They gave, "3s. 8d. in alms offering (for the relief of the poor) and 7s. 6d. for pittance for the abbot and convent (a donation to the Canons for food etc.) and the King dated letters patent at Beeleigh on the 10th", before leaving for Messing. Contrast this humble behaviour with the extreme actions, 250 years later, of one of Edward's successors, King Henry VIII. What impact did his orders have on the Holy Heart Shrine of Saint Roger Niger de Beeleigh?

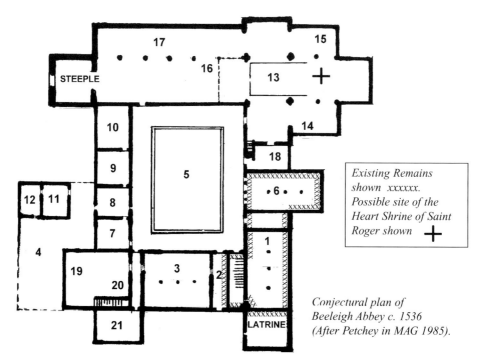

Existing Remains
shown *xxxxxx*.
Possible site of the
Heart Shrine of Saint
Roger shown **+**

Conjectural plan of
Beeleigh Abbey c. 1536
(After Petchey in MAG 1985).

KEY

1. Dorter Undercroft or Warming House (ground) and
   Dormitory or 'Great Chamber' (above)
2. Children's Chamber (above).
3. Dining Parlour or Refectory/Frater (above).
4. Possible site of the Outer Court or Yard (ground).
5. Cloister (ground).
6. Chapter House (ground).
7. Chamber (ground) and 'The White Chamber' (above).
8. Stairway space and chest store (ground and above).
9. Servant's Chambers (ground and above).
10. 'Another Chamber' (ground) and 'The Green Chamber' (above).
11. Bakehouse (ground).
12. Brewhouse (ground).
13. Church - Canons' Choir (ground).
14. Church - Our Lady Chapel (ground).
15. Church - Jesus Chapel (ground)
16. Church - St. Katherine's Chapel (ground).
17. Church - Rood Chapel in North Aisle (ground)
18. Vestry (ground)
19. Kitchen (ground)
20. Buttery (ground)
21. Infirmary or 'The Fermory Chamber' (ground).

15. DISSOLUTION AND DESTRUCTION

The Heart Shrine must have survived at Beeleigh Abbey for almost 300 years, continuing to generate income and devotion from countless numbers of visitors. Then, in 1536, it all came to an abrupt and very final end. King Henry VIII had severed most of the ties between the English Church and Rome and his vicar general Thomas Cromwell, promised to make him the richest prince in Christendom. The religious houses offered a vulnerable prize and in 1535, an enquiry was instituted into the numbers, wealth and revenue of all the monasteries. The results of this enquiry were collated and became known as the 'Valor Ecclesiasticus', a vast and very accurate assessment of the state of the religious houses there for the picking.

On some real and more fraudulent evidence the smaller foundations - that is those with an annual income of less than £200 - were suppressed by an act of parliament in 1536. In Essex, 23 houses fell into this category, including Beeleigh Abbey, which had an income at that stage of between £157 and £196 per annum. There was no general act dealing with the disposal of shrines and relics, although the King made it clear that; ".....the images and bones of such as (the people) restored and offered unto with ornaments of the same (should) be taken away.....". The destruction of shrines was carried out by the local commissioners responsible for the general closure of an Abbey or Priory and amongst other things, they "disgarnished" and disposed of bones, images, icons, relics and the like. Their overall aim was to prevent any such item from becoming the object of "renewed superstition and veneration".

The commissioners, Sir John St. Clere, Humphrey Brown, sergeant at law, Francis Jobson and Thomas Mildmay, arrived at Beeleigh and an inventory was taken on the 6th. June 1536. Rather curiously it appears to have been only partly completed as there are obvious omissions and a complete section of the Indenture was kept separate and delivered to the Abbot because he was to remain responsible for "certain parcels of goods and chattels....". The Earl of Essex in a letter to Cromwell on the 13th. January of the following year thanked him for ".....the goodness shewyd unto the abbot of Beyle prayeng you to conteynew your goodnes unto hym......". What was meant by this is unclear. The inventory certainly included items found in the Abbey Church not least; ".....a table of alabaster at the high alter praysed at.....", its reredos, hangings, brass and gilt copper cross and candlesticks, but there is absolutely no mention of any associated shrine, casket, relic, or anything else loosely associated with Saint Roger.

So what happened to Roger's heart? Perhaps it had been destroyed sometime between 1534 and 1536, as were most relics in England. However, a persistent local tradition has it that shortly before the commissioners arrived, the object was spirited away by the Canons and secretly conveyed and concealed in a place known only to them. This is not as far fetched as it may at first appear, as exactly the same was said to have happened at Durham, where the remains of Saint Cuthbert were allegedly recovered and hidden by Benedictine Monks. Perhaps, like those desperate Benedictines, the Beeleigh brethren hoped that the religious and political climate would change and that they would be able to restore the heart to its rightful place, near the high altar, but that was not to be. Things did not change and even the altar was sold for 13s. 4d. The Abbey buildings were also disposed of, being leased on the 8th January 1537 to John Gate of Garnetts, High Easter. Gate eventually purchased the property outright on the 15th., July 1540, for £300. The last Abbot, John Copsheffe, and the remaining Canons were pensioned off (the Abbot at £18 per annum) and as far as we know, the Holy relic of Saint Roger has not been seen or heard of since.

16. THE FACE OF THE SAINT?

Just fifty-five years after the Dissolution in March 1591, a curious case went before the authorities at the Maldon Sessions. The incident is recorded in volume 16 of the "Essex Review", however it can be summarised as follows. Edmund Hunt, a Maldon Inn Keeper, stood accused of contravening an earlier statute of 1563 which expressly directed "against Conjuracions, Inchantments and Witchecrafts". It was alleged that Hunt had been overheard talking with others at the White Hart Inn, at Fullbridge, Maldon, regarding treasure "hydd in the grownde.....about Byelie". It was said that he even produced a crude map "wherin were wrytten manye crosses....." and previously, via a third party called Thomas Collyne, had a "peece of ye earth" from Beeleigh analysed by the infamous mystic and astrologer, Dr. Dee. It was decided that Hunt should be bound over and ordered to appear at the next Sessions, but the sequel to this story has not survived.

Floor tile fragment (c.1290 - 1350), found at Beeleigh Abbey; a product of the 'Westminster Tiler'.

What was Hunt looking for? Why was he convinced, to the very point of breaking the law, that something precious was buried at Beeleigh? Was he searching for booty hidden by the Canons? Did that treasure allegedly include an elusive gold and jewelled relic casket? We will probably never know, but small clues, albeit not of any intrinsic value, have surfaced in the area. A floor tile fragment, of a Lion in a Trellis Pattern, has been discovered in an area thought to have been some kind of loading-bay, for the removal of hundreds of bricks and other building materials by barge at the time of the Abbey's closure. The tile is a product of the so-called 'Westminster Tiler' and was made in the London area. It dates from the late-thirteenth to the middle-fourteenth century (c.1290-1350) a period when the Heart Shrine was definitely located in the Abbey and, enhanced by the recent Royal visit, the place was doubtless enjoying enough income to be able to beautify the Church with a new floor-surface. A lead 'Ampulla', or pilgrim flask, has also been found within the supposed site of the Outer-Court. It was originally designed to contain a dose of thaumaturgic water dispensed at a shrine. Was it, in this case, at the shrine of St. Roger?

Nothing has been discovered so far, however, that can be directly associated with Roger Niger. His later tomb, cushion and cape were destroyed during the Great Fire at St. Paul's. His gold ring has not been heard of since Hatfield Priory was dissolved and the Beeleigh Heart Relic has similarly disappeared without trace. The Abbey itself has been largely demolished, although the surviving remains are of great interest. They consist of the east and south-east parts of the building adjoining the cloister - the Chapter House, Parlour, Dorter/Dormitory, associated Dorter Undercroft or Warming House, and elements of the Refectory/Frater and Rere-Dorter/Latrine. All largely date from the first half of the thirteenth-century, with the exception of a later, sixteenth-century, timber-framed addition. The Church has been completely destroyed, even its foundations were grubbed up during gravel extraction in the nineteenth-century, and the site of the high altar and shrine are now under the deep waters of an ornamental lake/duck-pond.

Lead ampulla or pilgrim flask found at Beeleigh.

Inside the Abbey remains are seven small panels of painted glass. They, too, have had a chequered past. Made sometime during the first half of the fifteenth-century, they were removed to Maldon Hall early in the nineteenth-century and returned to the Abbey during the 1920s. One of the panels is of a sainted bishop, vested in chasuble, dalmatic and alb, with mitre and pastoral staff and with his right hand raised in benediction. The figure stands on a pedestal labelled 'Augustin', but the figure and pedestal do not match each other. The bottom of the pastoral staff is not in line with the rest of it and the dress is certainly not that of Saint Augustine. So who is it? Writing in 1922, Rev. Canon Galpin, then President of the Essex Archaeological Society, was quite clear - he believed that it was intended to represent Saint Roger.

Is this then the image of Roger Niger de Beeleigh? Can we still gaze on the face of the Saint? If so, this must surely be the strangest and most awe inspiring survival of a most remarkable man.

> ".....This Roger was a reverend man, religious, learned,
> painful in preaching, eloquent a great house-keeper,
> of very gentle and courteous behaviour (saieth Matthew Paris)....
> whereunto it might be added that he was also stout and couragious.....".
>   Francis Godwin.
>   "Succession of the Bishops of England".

Is this a depiction of St. Roger? The label on the pedestal says 'Augustin', but Canon Galpin thought it was more likely to be Roger Niger.

45

SELECT BIBLIOGRAPHY

MANUSCRIPT SOURCES

London: The Public Record Office
C53/30. Statutes of the Realm, 21 Henry 111. Carta Confirmationis.

Cambridge University Library
MS Gg.4.32,ff. 117r-124v. Collection of Statutes for the Rectors and Priests of the Archdeaconry of St. Roger.

Bull of Pope Boniface IX (22/7/1391)
Calendar of entries in the Papal Registers relating to Great Britain and Ireland (Papal Letters. Vol.4, pg.399).

PRINTED SOURCES

Bottomly, F. Abbeys, Monasteries and Churches of Great Britain. 1981.
Brandon, A. Human Heart - The Holy Relic of Beeleigh Abbey. E.C.N. 21.7.2000
Buckler, G. Twenty-Two of the Churches of Essex. 1856.
Butler, J. The Quest for Becket's Bones. 1995.
Chancellor, F. St. Thomas the Apostle, Navestock. ER (vol. 4). 1895.
Clark, Rev. A. Buried Treasure at Beeleigh Abbey. ER (vol. 16). 1907.
Colchester, D. An Essex Saint: Saint Roger Niger. EC (no.52). 1956.
Drayton, M. Poly-Olbion. 1612 & 1622.
Dugdale, Sir W. The History of St. Paul's Cathedral. 1658.
Fitch, E.A. Maldon and the River Blackwater. 1894.
Fowler, R.C. The Abbey of Beeleigh by Maldon. VCH (vol.2). 1907.
Fowler, R.C. (Editor). Beeleigh Abbey. 1922.
Fowler, R.C. Essex Chapels. TEAS (vol.XVI). 1923.
Galpin, Rev. Canon. St. Roger's Ring. ER (vol.30).1921.
Gardiner, J. & Wenborn N. (Editors). The History Today Companion to British History. 1995.
Gasquet F.A. (Editor). Collectanea Anglo-Prernonstratensia. CS. 1904-1906.
Gibbs, M. (Editor). Early Charters of the Cathedral Church of St. Paul, London. RHS. 1939.
Godwin, F. The succession of the bishops of England. TPL. 1625.
Grabois, A. Medieval Civilisation. 1980.
Gregory Nicholson, A.J. Beeleigh Abbey 750th Anniversary Drama – A Play. 1930.
Gregory Nicholson, A.J. St. Roger his Ring - A Play. 1934.
Hardie, A. The heart surgeon - on Robert the Bruce. DMN. 3/9/1996.
Harding, A. England in the Thirteenth Century. 1993.
Hennessy, Rev. G. Novurn Repertorium Ecclesiasticum Parochiale Londinense. 1898.
Holland, H. Ecelesia Sancti Pauli Illustrata. 1633.
Hughes, Rev. L. A Guide to the Church of All Saints, Maldon. 1909.
Kingsford, C.L. Roger Niger de Bileye. DNB (vol.XIV). 1909.

Printed Sources (continued)

Kirk R.E.G. (Editor). Feet of Fines for Essex - Vol. 1 (1182-1272) EAS. 1899 - 1910.
Lawrence, C.H. The Life of Saint Edmund by Matthew Paris. 1996.
Newcourt R. Repertorium ecclesiasticum parochiale Londinense. TPL. 1708-10.
Nunn, S.P. Beeleigh Ancient Hamlet. 1982.
Nunn, S.P. Heart of St. Roger. ECM. June 1989.
Nunn, S.P. Almost Maldon's Patron Saint. MBN. 1/2/1990.
Ousby, I. The Cambridge Guide to Literature in English. 1988.
Paris, Matthew. Historia major. TPL. 1640.
Petchey, W.J. Beeleigh Abbey in 1536. MAG. 1985.
Petchey, W.J. A Prospect of Maldon (1500-1689).1991.
Pevsner, N. The Buildings of England - Essex. 1954.
Powicke, M. The Thirteenth Century (1216-1307). 1953.
Reaney, P.H. The Origin of English Surnames. 1967.
Reaney, P.H. The Place Names of Essex. 1969.
Round, J.H. The Heart of St. Roger. TEAS (vol.XVI). 1923.
Simpson, J.A. & Weiner, E.S.C. (Eds). Oxford English Dictionary. (2nd. Edition. Vol.2). 1999.
Smith, H. Roger of Beeleigh. ER (vol.XXXVIII). 1929.
Sox, D. Relics and Shrines. 1985.
Sparrow-Simpson, W. Documents Illustrating the History of St. Paul's Cathedral. CS. 1880.
Stenton, F.M. John Horace Round (1854-1928). DNB. 1922-1930.
Vaughan, R. (Editor). The Illustrated Chronicles of Matthew Paris. 1993.
Ward, G.A. Victorian and Edwardian Brentwood. 1980.
Weever, J. Ancient funeral monuments. TPL. 1631.
Weinreb, B. & Hibbert, C. (Editors). The London Encyclopaedia. 1983.
Wharton, H. Historia de episcopis et decanis Londinensibus. TPL. 1695.
Whitfield, J.L. St. Roger of Beeleigh. BDM. (no.9). Nov.1922.

Key

BDM = Brentwood Diocesan Magazine
CS = Camden Society
DMN = Daily Mail Newspaper
DNB = Dictionary of National Biography
EAS = Essex Archaeological Society
EC = The Essex Churchman
ECM = Essex Countryside Magazine
ECN = Essex Chronicle Newspaper
ER = Essex Review
MAG = Maldon Archaeological Group. Ecclesiastical Monuments of Maldon Project
MBN = Maldon and Burnham Standard Newspaper
TEAS = Transactions of the Essex Archaeological Society (New Series)
TPL = The copy consulted is held in Thomas Plume's Library, Maldon
RHS = Royal Historical Society
VCH = Victoria County History of Essex

Other publications by Maldon Archaeological and Historical Group.
(Formerly Maldon Archaeological Group)

The Carmelite Friary at Maldon Essex, 1986.
Maeldune, Light on Maldon's Distant Past, 1992.
A History of Beeleigh Mill, 1997.
Underground Maldon, the cellars beneath the town, 1998.

These publications, with the exception of "Maeldune", are available from Maldon bookshops or from MAHG committee members.

Cover design and book layout by K.A.Cook.